JOSHUA
FROM START2FINISH

MICHAEL WHITWORTH

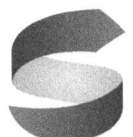

© 2025 by Start2Finish

All rights reserved. No part of this publication may be reproduced, stored in a retrieval system, or transmitted in any form or by any means without the prior written permission of the author. The only exception is brief quotations in printed reviews.

ISBN 978-1-941972-80-9

Published by Start2Finish
Bend, Oregon 97702
start2finish.org

Printed in the United States of America

Unless otherwise noted, all Scripture quotations are from The Holy Bible, English Standard Version®, copyright © 2001 by Crossway Bibles, a publishing ministry of Good News Publishers. Used by permission. All rights reserved.

Cover Design: Evangela Creative

CONTENTS

1.	Be Strong & Courageous	5
2.	A Woman of Faith	13
3.	Crossing the Jordan	21
4.	Preparing for Battle	29
5.	The Fall of Jericho	37
6.	Sin in the Camp	45
7.	Victory at Ai	53
8.	The Gibeonite Deception	61
9.	The Long Day of Battle	69
10.	Rest from War	77
11.	The Land Divided	85
12.	The Altar of Witness	93
13.	Choose Whom You Will Serve	101

1

BE STRONG & COURAGEOUS

JOSHUA 1

Objective: To show that true courage and success come from trusting God's presence and obeying his word.

INTRODUCTION

On June 6, 1944, Allied troops stood on the edge of history. The beaches of Normandy stretched before them—five miles of sand, wire, and gunfire that would determine the course of the war. No one could guarantee success; many would not survive the day. Yet thousands pressed forward, driven by duty and faith in a cause greater than themselves. In that moment, courage meant advancing into the unknown, trusting that victory was possible.

Joshua faced a similar threshold. After forty years in the wilderness, Israel camped beside the Jordan River, gazing toward the land God had promised. Moses, their great leader, was gone. Ahead lay fortified cities, fierce enemies, and battles they had never fought. But the Lord's word was clear: "Arise, go over this Jordan." Joshua's story teaches that courage does not come from confidence in ourselves but from confidence in the God who keeps his promises.

EXAMINATION

God commissions Joshua (1:1-9)

The book of Joshua opens with a solemn transition: "After the death of Moses the servant of the Lord, the Lord said to Joshua the son of Nun, Moses' assistant, 'Moses my servant is dead. Now therefore arise, go over this Jordan, you and all this people, into the land that I am giving to them, to the people of Israel'" (1:1-2). These opening words remind us that God's work continues even when his servants pass away. Moses had been Israel's deliverer, lawgiver, and mediator for forty years. Yet his death did not end God's promises. Leadership changes; divine faithfulness does not. The book begins with both grief and resolve—the old generation had died in the wilderness, but the new stood ready to enter Canaan.

Joshua had served Moses faithfully for decades. He was the military commander during the battle with Amalek (Exod. 17:8-16), one of the twelve spies who had believed God's promise (Num. 14:6-9), and Moses' assistant throughout the wilderness years. When Moses laid hands on Joshua (Num. 27:18-23), he was publicly commissioned as the one who would lead Israel into the promised land. Now the moment had come. The Lord's command was simple yet staggering: "Arise, go over this Jordan." What the nation had long awaited was finally at hand.

God immediately assured Joshua of his promise: "Every place that the sole of your foot will tread upon I have given to you, just as I promised to Moses" (1:3). The extent of the land is described in verse 4—from the wilderness in the south to Lebanon in the north, from the Euphrates River to the Great Sea in the west. The boundaries echo the original promise to Abraham (Gen. 15:18-21), reminding Joshua that this conquest was the fulfillment of ancient covenant oaths. Yet the land was not a gift apart from effort. Israel would have to fight, trust, and obey. God would give victory, but only as his people acted in faith.

The Lord also gave Joshua a personal assurance: "No man shall be able to stand before you all the days of your life. Just as I was with Moses, so I will be with you. I will not leave you or forsake you" (1:5). These words echo the same promise given to Moses in Exodus 3:12 and later repeated to all believers in Hebrews 13:5. Joshua's success would depend not on military strategy or numerical strength but on God's abiding presence. The same God who parted the Red Sea, sent manna from heaven, and dwelt in the tabernacle would now go before him.

Three times in verses 6–9, God tells Joshua, "Be strong and courageous." The repetition underlines both Joshua's fear and God's grace. Courage would not come from self-confidence but from confidence in the Lord's promise. In verse 6, Joshua must be strong because God would give the land to Israel. In verse 7, he must be strong to obey the law of Moses. And in verse 9, he must be strong because the Lord is with him wherever he goes. Strength of faith and courage of obedience always go together.

In verses 7–8, God links Joshua's success directly to his devotion to Scripture: "Be careful to do according to all the law that Moses my servant commanded you. Do not turn from it to the right hand or to the left … This Book of the Law shall not depart from your mouth, but you shall meditate on it day and night." The leader of Israel was to be a man of God's word. Victory in battle and prosperity in life would come only through obedience. The same principle still holds true for Christians: spiritual success flows from a heart rooted in God's word (Psa. 1:2–3; Jas. 1:25).

God concludes this section with a question and a command that resound through the ages: "Have I not commanded you? Be strong and courageous. Do not be frightened, and do not be dismayed, for the Lord your God is with you wherever you go" (1:9). Joshua could face the unknown because he was not alone. Israel's victories would not come from human might but divine presence. The heart of this chapter—and indeed the whole book—is the truth that faith in God's promises produces courage to obey his commands.

Joshua commands the people (1:10–18)

Having received his commission, Joshua immediately moved to action. Biblical faith never leads to passivity. "And Joshua commanded the officers of the people, 'Pass through the midst of the camp and command the people, "Prepare your provisions, for within three days you are to pass over this Jordan to go in to take possession of the land that the Lord your God is giving you to possess"'" (1:10–11). The emphasis again falls on divine initiative—"the Lord your God is giving you"—and human responsibility—"prepare your provisions." God's promises demand our participation. Joshua's leadership displays quiet confidence; he did not call for a vote or a committee but simply relayed the Lord's instruction.

Next Joshua turned his attention to the tribes of Reuben, Gad, and the half-tribe of Manasseh (1:12-15). These groups had already received their inheritance on the east side of the Jordan (Num. 32:1-33), but they had pledged to help their brothers conquer the land west of the river. Joshua reminded them of their commitment: "Remember the word that Moses the servant of the Lord commanded you ... all the men of valor among you shall pass over armed before your brothers and shall help them" (1:13-14). Though they had settled comfortably, they were not exempt from service. God's people are bound together in shared purpose; no tribe could rest while others struggled.

The unity of Israel is striking. Twelve tribes, scattered across varied regions and temperaments, would cross together as one nation. Their cooperation anticipates the unity Christ desires for his church (John 17:20-23). Just as Reuben, Gad, and Manasseh were to aid their brethren, so Christians are called to bear one another's burdens (Gal. 6:2). God's victories are communal, not individual.

The people's response to Joshua reveals their faith and submission: "And they answered Joshua, 'All that you have commanded us we will do, and wherever you send us we will go. Just as we obeyed Moses in all things, so we will obey you. Only may the Lord your God be with you, as he was with Moses!'" (1:16-17). The Israelites recognized that Joshua's authority derived from God's presence, not personal ambition. They prayed for the same divine companionship that had guided Moses.

The closing verse carries both encouragement and warning: "Whoever rebels against your commandment and disobeys your words, whatever you command him, shall be put to death. Only be strong and courageous" (1:18). These words echo God's earlier command, forming a literary and theological bookend. The success of Israel's mission would depend on courage rooted in obedience. The people pledged absolute loyalty to God's appointed leader, knowing that rebellion would bring ruin. Their charge to Joshua—"Only be strong and courageous"—shows that true leadership inspires confidence in others when it rests securely on God's word.

Themes and theological reflections

Several vital truths emerge from this opening chapter. First, ***God's promises are certain even when his servants change.*** The phrase "Moses my servant is dead" acknowledges the mortality of human leaders. Yet the covenant purposes of God march on. His faithfulness transcends generations, assuring believers that no transition can thwart his plan.

Second, *courage flows from confidence in God's presence*. Joshua's charge was not to summon inner bravery but to trust in divine companionship. The Lord did not promise an absence of danger, only the certainty of his nearness. Courage is not the lack of fear but faith that God is greater than our fear.

Third, *success in God's work depends on obedience to his word*. The repeated call to meditate on the law day and night underscores that victory begins in the heart before it is seen on the battlefield. God's leader must be a student of Scripture. In every generation, spiritual strength grows from devotion to the Word that reveals the will of God.

Fourth, *unity among God's people is essential to fulfilling his mission*. The cooperation of the eastern tribes demonstrates that obedience is not merely personal but collective. Israel would conquer together or fail together. The church today faces the same truth: we share one mission, one Lord, and one faith.

Finally, *leadership in God's kingdom requires both strength and submission*. Joshua's authority came from his willingness to obey God's voice. He led decisively because he followed faithfully. The chapter begins with God's command to "be strong and courageous" and ends with the people echoing it back to their leader—a fitting reminder that courage is both commanded and confirmed within the community of faith.

APPLICATION

1. God's work continues

Moses' death reminds us that no servant is indispensable to God's purposes. When one leader's work ends, another's begins. The kingdom never depends on a single person; it depends on the Lord who remains ever faithful. Christians must resist the temptation to tie their hope to human figures—preachers, elders, or teachers. God's plan moves forward through changing generations and imperfect people. Like Joshua, we are called to rise and serve when God says, "Arise, go over this Jordan." Faith steps forward even when the shoes we fill seem too large.

2. Strength through Scripture

God's command to Joshua to meditate on the law day and night reveals that courage and obedience spring from God's word. Spiritual strength does not come from personality, experience, or emotion but from continual reflection on Scripture. When the word shapes our thoughts, it steadies our hearts. Christians who keep God's word on their lips and in their minds will find the courage to face temptation, grief, and uncertainty. Every victory in the book of Joshua flowed from faith rooted in revelation. The same is true today—our success in God's work depends on knowing and doing what he has spoken.

3. Courage through presence

The Lord's promise, "I will not leave you or forsake you," remains one of the most comforting truths in Scripture. Joshua could lead boldly because he knew God was near. Christians share that same assurance through Christ's presence: "Behold, I am with you always, to the end of the age" (Matt. 28:20). Courage grows when we remember we never walk alone. Whether confronting sin, standing for truth, or enduring hardship, we find confidence in the God who goes before us. Our task is not to summon fearless hearts but to trust the One who is always faithful.

4. Unity in mission

Joshua reminded the eastern tribes of their promise to help their brothers. God's people could not enjoy rest while others still battled. The same spirit of unity must shape the church today. We cannot be content while others struggle in faith or stand outside the grace of God. Christians are bound together by a shared mission to help one another reach the promised rest. We bear one another's burdens, serve each other in love, and labor side by side until all God's people have entered their inheritance.

CONCLUSION

The opening chapter of Joshua sets the tone for the entire book. God's promises are sure, his presence is constant, and his word is the foundation of every victory. Joshua's call to "be strong and courageous" was not a slogan for battle but a summons to faith. As believers face transitions, uncertainties, and spiritual challenges, the same command still speaks: strength is found in obedience, courage in trust, and success in walking with the Lord. The God who parted the Jordan for Israel continues to lead his people into the blessings he has promised.

REFLECTION

1. What does God's faithfulness through changing leaders teach you about his unchanging nature?

2. How does Joshua's example help you face new responsibilities or uncertain seasons?

3. What does it mean for Scripture to "not depart from your mouth"?

4. In what areas do you most need courage to obey God's word?

5. How can remembering God's presence strengthen you in daily struggles?

6. What promises of God encourage you when fear or doubt arises?

DISCUSSION

1. Why do you think God repeated "be strong and courageous" three times?

2. How can leaders today model Joshua's devotion to God's word?

3. What parallels exist between Israel's unity in conquest and the church's mission today?

4. Why is obedience to Scripture essential to spiritual success?

5. What does Joshua 1 reveal about the relationship between divine sovereignty and human effort?

6. How can we help one another "cross the Jordan" moments of faith in our lives?

2

A WOMAN OF FAITH
JOSHUA 2

Objective: To affirm that genuine faith trusts God's promises, acts courageously, and welcomes his grace.

INTRODUCTION

In 1940, as German bombs rained down on London, a young woman named Mary Jones refused to flee her city. Night after night, she helped guide neighbors to safety, offering them food, blankets, and courage. Her small acts of faith saved lives in the darkness. Years later, when asked why she stayed, she said simply, "I trusted that God would be near, even in the worst of nights."

Rahab's story echoes that same kind of faith—a courage born not of certainty in circumstances but of confidence in God. When two Israelite spies entered Jericho, she chose to hide them at great personal risk. She had only heard of Israel's God, yet she believed his power and mercy were real. Her rooftop decision changed the course of her life and became a testimony of grace that endures through Scripture.

Joshua 2 invites us to see faith through the eyes of a Gentile woman who dared to trust in a God she had never met. Through Rahab, we learn that faith is not limited by background, gender, or past sin. The Lord welcomes all who come to him in trust, and he delights to turn unlikely hearts into shining examples of belief.

EXAMINATION

The spies enter Jericho (2:1-7)

The story of Rahab begins quietly but carries enormous theological weight. "And Joshua the son of Nun sent two men secretly from Shittim as spies, saying, 'Go, view the land, especially Jericho'" (2:1). Jericho was the first major obstacle in Israel's conquest of Canaan—a walled city guarding the approaches from the Jordan Valley into the hill country beyond. The spies' mission recalls the earlier scouting expedition in Numbers 13, but with one crucial difference: this time, faith would triumph where fear once failed.

The men entered Jericho and "came into the house of a prostitute whose name was Rahab and lodged there." Ancient inns were often places of both lodging and immorality, so it is not surprising that Rahab's home served as a natural gathering point for travelers. The text never excuses her sin but highlights the surprising grace of God, who works through unlikely people to accomplish his purposes. Rahab, a Canaanite woman with a shameful occupation, would become the first citizen of Jericho to confess faith in the Lord and later appear in the genealogy of Jesus (Matt. 1:5).

Word of the spies quickly reached the king of Jericho: "Behold, men of Israel have come here tonight to search out the land." Jericho's ruler sent an urgent command for Rahab to surrender the intruders. Instead, she hid the men under stalks of flax on her roof and misled the soldiers: "True, the men came to me, but I did not know where they were from. And when the gate was about to be closed at dark, the men went out. Pursue them quickly, for you will overtake them" (2:4-5).

Rahab's deception has raised moral questions for generations. Scripture does not praise her lie, but it does commend her faith. Hebrews 11:31 and James 2:25 both celebrate Rahab's trust and action, not her dishonesty. Her decision reflected the limited moral understanding of someone newly coming to faith, acting in crisis to protect God's messengers. She risked her life for the sake of the Lord's people—a sign of a heart already turning toward him.

The soldiers searched the road to the fords of the Jordan while the gates of Jericho were shut. Meanwhile, the spies remained hidden on

Rahab's roof, protected by her courage and quick thinking. The scene contrasts Jericho's fear with Rahab's faith. The king relied on walls and weapons; Rahab relied on the word of a God she had only heard about.

Rahab's confession of faith (2:8–14)

Before the spies lay down to sleep, Rahab came to them on the roof and spoke words that reveal a remarkable understanding of God's power and promise. "I know that the Lord has given you the land," she said, "and that the fear of you has fallen upon us, and that all the inhabitants of the land melt away before you" (2:9). Her confession begins with certainty—"I know." Though a pagan woman in a doomed city, Rahab believed what Israel's God had declared. She interpreted the news of Israel's victories not as political developments but as divine acts.

Rahab recalled two specific events: "For we have heard how the Lord dried up the water of the Red Sea before you when you came out of Egypt, and what you did to the two kings of the Amorites who were beyond the Jordan, to Sihon and Og" (2:10). Those miracles had occurred forty years earlier, yet their reputation had not faded. The Canaanites knew of the Lord's power, but only Rahab responded with faith. Knowledge alone does not save; it must lead to trust and surrender.

Her next words show both fear and reverence: "As soon as we heard it, our hearts melted, and there was no spirit left in any man because of you, for the Lord your God, he is God in the heavens above and on the earth beneath" (2:11). This is one of the strongest confessions of faith in the Old Testament. Rahab, once an idolater, recognized the Lord as the true and universal God. Her statement echoes the great confession of Deuteronomy 4:39 and anticipates the Gentile faith later welcomed in the gospel.

Rahab then pleaded for mercy: "Now then, please swear to me by the Lord that, as I have dealt kindly with you, you also will deal kindly with my father's house" (2:12). The word "kindly" translates *hesed*—covenant faithfulness or steadfast love. Rahab, though outside Israel, appealed to the very character of God's covenant mercy. She sought protection not only for herself but for her entire household. True faith always cares about the salvation of others.

The spies agreed: "Our life for yours even to death! … When the Lord gives us the land we will deal kindly and faithfully with you" (2:14). Their reply confirmed that Israel's coming victory was certain and that Rahab's faith would not go unrewarded. The covenant of mercy was sealed by oath.

The sign of the scarlet cord (2:15-21)

Rahab helped the spies escape through a window in the city wall: "She let them down by a rope through the window, for her house was built into the city wall." The architecture of Jericho allowed for houses within the outer defenses, offering both opportunity and danger. She instructed the men to hide in the hill country for three days until the pursuers returned, demonstrating practical wisdom as well as faith.

The spies, however, required a sign to mark her household for deliverance: "Behold, when we come into the land, you shall tie this scarlet cord in the window through which you let us down, and you shall gather into your house your father and mother, your brothers, and all your father's household" (2:18). Anyone inside Rahab's house under the sign of the cord would be spared; anyone outside would perish. The scarlet cord thus became a visible emblem of faith and obedience.

Throughout Christian history, interpreters have seen typological meaning in this symbol. The scarlet color recalls the blood of the Passover lamb that marked Israelite homes in Egypt (Exod. 12:7, 13). In both cases, deliverance came through faith in God's promise and the sign of blood. The New Testament later connects Rahab's faith with salvation through Christ's sacrifice (Heb. 11:31). Her trust in the Lord foreshadowed the redemption offered to all who take refuge in him.

Rahab responded with immediate obedience: "According to your words, so be it." She tied the scarlet cord in her window, declaring by her actions what she had already confessed with her lips. Faith that saves is faith that acts (Jas. 2:25-26). Rahab did not wait until the army arrived to decide where her loyalty lay; she had already chosen Jehovah over Jericho.

The spies return to Joshua (2:22-24)

After hiding for three days in the hills, the spies safely crossed the Jordan and returned to Joshua. They brought a report far different from the one their predecessors had given in Numbers 13. "Truly the Lord has given all the land into our hands," they said, "and also, all the inhabitants of the land melt away because of us" (2:24). The faith of one Canaanite woman had strengthened the faith of Israel's entire leadership.

This reversal highlights the transformative power of belief. Forty years earlier, ten spies had demoralized the nation with their fear; now two spies inspired confidence through Rahab's testimony. Faith begets faith. When we see God working in unexpected places, our own trust grows stronger.

Rahab's story stands as a monument to divine grace. She was not an Israelite, not morally pure, not religiously educated. Yet she believed that the Lord was God and acted on that belief. Her faith crossed cultural, moral, and national boundaries, revealing that God's mercy reaches far beyond the expected.

Theological reflections

The narrative of Joshua 2 illustrates several vital themes. First, *God's grace welcomes the outsider.* Rahab's inclusion in Israel—and later in the Messianic line—demonstrates that God's salvation is not limited by ancestry or past sin. The Lord delights to redeem those the world overlooks.

Second, *true faith combines belief and action.* Rahab's confession alone would not have saved her had she not acted to protect the spies and display the scarlet cord. James cites her example to teach that genuine faith manifests itself in works of obedience.

Third, *God uses unlikely instruments to accomplish his will.* The conquest of Canaan began not with a warrior's sword but with a woman's faith. Her rooftop courage prepared the way for Jericho's fall. God often chooses the weak to shame the strong, that no one may boast before him (1 Cor. 1:27–29).

Finally, *Rahab's story foreshadows redemption through Christ.* The scarlet cord points to the blood of Jesus, through which sinners from every nation find refuge. Like Rahab, we are saved not by status or heritage but by trusting the promise of mercy and sheltering beneath its sign.

APPLICATION

1. Faith that risks

Rahab's decision to hide the spies was an act of extraordinary risk. She endangered her own life because she trusted the Lord's promise more than Jericho's power. Faith always requires stepping beyond safety and convenience. Christians are called to obey even when obedience brings cost or conflict. Like Rahab, we must decide which kingdom we belong to—the city of man or the kingdom of God. Every act of courageous faith, whether small or great, declares our loyalty to the Lord who saves.

2. God's grace reaches outsiders

Rahab's story proves that no one is beyond the reach of divine mercy. A Canaanite prostitute became a model of faith and an ancestor of the Messiah. Her redemption reminds believers that God's grace can transform any past. The gospel still calls outsiders in—from sin to salvation, from shame to service. Christians must extend that same open welcome to others, trusting that God can redeem lives the world has written off. The church is strongest when it remembers it was built by grace, not by merit.

3. Faith that acts

Rahab's belief was proven by her obedience. She tied the scarlet cord in her window and gathered her family inside. Genuine faith always produces visible commitment. Words of belief must become works of faithfulness. Christians today demonstrate trust through repentance, worship, and daily obedience. As Rahab's family found safety under the sign of faith, so believers find salvation under the blood of Christ. Trust that acts brings life; profession without obedience leaves destruction.

4. Faith that strengthens others

Rahab's courage encouraged the spies, whose report strengthened Joshua and all Israel. Faith is contagious; one believer's trust can rekindle the hope of many. In times of fear or fatigue, the example of a faithful heart reminds the church that God still works mightily. Our quiet acts of faith may inspire others more than we know. When we stand firm for God, we help others do the same. Rahab's faith changed her destiny and uplifted an entire nation's confidence.

CONCLUSION

Rahab's faith shines like a light in the darkness of Canaan. She believed when others trembled, acted when others hesitated, and received mercy when others perished. Her story reminds us that faith is not about heritage or worthiness but about trusting the living God who saves. The scarlet cord hanging from her window testified to that trust—a vivid sign that salvation belongs to those who trust and obey. Through Rahab's faith, God revealed his heart for the nations and foreshadowed the redemption found in Christ. Her example challenges every believer to act boldly on what we know of God's promises and to welcome others into the refuge of his grace.

REFLECTION

1. What makes Rahab's faith remarkable in light of her background?
2. How does her story challenge your view of who God can use?
3. Why is it important that Rahab acted on her belief rather than only confessing it?
4. What does the scarlet cord symbolize for Christians today?
5. How has someone else's faith strengthened your own?
6. Where is God calling you to trust him courageously right now?

DISCUSSION

1. How does Rahab's confession in verse 11 compare to Israel's unbelief in Numbers 13?
2. What lessons does Rahab's story teach about God's mission to the nations?
3. Why does James cite Rahab as an example of living faith?
4. In what ways does Rahab's faith foreshadow the gospel of Christ?
5. How can the church better reflect God's grace to those with troubled pasts?
6. What modern "Jerichos" require us to act with Rahab's kind of courage?

3

CROSSING THE JORDAN

JOSHUA 3-4

Objective: To demonstrate that faith moves forward, trusting God's presence to make a way through obstacles.

INTRODUCTION

In 1859, engineer Charles Blondin amazed the world by walking across Niagara Falls on a tightrope. Crowds gathered on both sides of the gorge as he carried out daring stunts—crossing blindfolded, on stilts, even pushing a wheelbarrow. After one performance, Blondin asked the spectators if they believed he could carry a person across. They shouted "Yes!" But when he asked for a volunteer, silence fell. Everyone believed, but no one trusted enough to step forward.

Israel stood at a similar moment of decision beside the flooded Jordan. They had heard of God's power, seen his wonders in the wilderness, and received his promises—but now they had to act. The river would not part until faith took a step. Joshua's command, "Arise, go over this Jordan," tested their trust and proved that victory always begins with obedience.

The crossing of the Jordan is more than an ancient miracle; it is a timeless lesson in faith. Every Christian faces moments when God calls us to move forward into uncertainty. Like Israel, we must fix our eyes on his presence, consecrate our hearts, and step into the waters of obedience, trusting that he will make a way.

EXAMINATION

Preparation for the crossing (3:1–6)

Early the next morning, Joshua led Israel from Shittim to the banks of the Jordan River. The people had waited forty years for this moment, but one great obstacle remained—the river itself. "At this time of year the Jordan overflows all its banks" (3:15). What seemed like a natural barrier was in truth an opportunity for God to display his power. Joshua and the nation camped near the river for three days, facing the impossible and waiting for God's direction.

The officers then went through the camp with clear instructions: "When you see the ark of the covenant of the Lord your God being carried by the Levitical priests, then you shall set out from your place and follow it" (3:3). The ark symbolized the Lord's presence, his covenant, and his rule among the people. Israel's success depended on keeping their eyes on the ark—on the Lord himself—rather than on the river. The officers added, "There shall be a distance between you and it, about two thousand cubits in length. Do not come near it, in order that you may know the way you shall go" (3:4). The sacred distance reinforced reverence for God's holiness and dependence on his guidance.

Joshua told the people, "Consecrate yourselves, for tomorrow the Lord will do wonders among you" (3:5). The command to consecrate likely involved washing garments and abstaining from impurity (Exod. 19:10–15). But its deeper meaning was spiritual: prepare your hearts for God's mighty work. Before victory, there must be holiness. The Lord's wonders are reserved for those who approach him with clean hands and pure hearts.

Joshua also spoke to the priests, saying, "Take up the ark of the covenant and pass on before the people" (3:6). The priests would lead the way into the river, demonstrating that God's presence, not human strength, would open the path to Canaan. Every movement of Israel's camp was centered on the ark—a visible sign that the Lord himself was leading them forward.

The Lord exalts Joshua (3:7–13)

The Lord then confirmed Joshua's leadership: "Today I will begin to exalt you in the sight of all Israel, that they may know that, as I was with Moses, so I will be with you" (3:7). Just as the Red Sea miracle had validated Moses' calling, the Jordan crossing would authenticate Joshua's. Leadership in God's kingdom is not established by human ambition but by divine presence and obedience.

Joshua instructed the priests, "When you come to the brink of the waters of the Jordan, you shall stand still in the Jordan" (3:8). Their act of faith would trigger the miracle. To the people, Joshua said, "Come here and listen to the words of the Lord your God" (3:9). He declared that the crossing would prove the living God was among them and that he would "without fail drive out from before you the Canaanites, the Hittites, the Hivites, the Perizzites, the Girgashites, the Amorites, and the Jebusites" (3:10). The phrase "the living God" emphasizes that Israel's God was active and powerful, unlike the idols of Canaan.

Joshua then gave specific details of the event: "Behold, the ark of the covenant of the Lord of all the earth is passing over before you into the Jordan" (3:11). God is not merely Israel's deity but "the Lord of all the earth." His sovereignty extends over nations, rivers, and nature itself. Joshua instructed twelve men—one from each tribe—to be chosen for a later purpose (3:12). The selection ensured that every tribe would share in remembering what God was about to do.

Finally, Joshua announced what would happen: "When the soles of the feet of the priests bearing the ark of the Lord ... shall rest in the waters of the Jordan, the waters of the Jordan shall be cut off ... and shall stand in one heap" (3:13). The miracle would come only when the priests stepped into the water. Faith sometimes must move forward before God acts.

The crossing of the Jordan (3:14–17)

The moment arrived. As the priests carrying the ark approached the river, the text stresses the timing: "The Jordan overflows all its banks throughout the time of harvest" (3:15). Crossing then was humanly impossible. Yet "when the feet of the priests bearing the ark were dipped in the brink of the water, the waters coming down from above stood and rose up in a heap very far away, at Adam, the city that is beside Zarethan" (3:15–16). The floodwaters stopped nearly twenty miles upstream, leaving a dry riverbed near Jericho.

This event mirrored the parting of the Red Sea (Exod. 14:21–22), marking the end of Israel's wilderness and the beginning of their life in the land of promise. Just as Israel had entered freedom through the sea, they now entered inheritance through the river. The priests stood "firmly on dry ground in the midst of the Jordan, and all Israel was passing over on dry ground until all the nation finished passing over the Jordan" (3:17).

The miracle's purpose was twofold: to reveal God's power and to call his people to faith. Only when the priests obeyed did the waters part. The Lord honors obedient trust. Christians today experience the same principle—God works mightily when his people step forward in faith, confident that his promises will hold.

Memorial stones from the river (4:1–9)

After the crossing, God commanded Joshua to establish a memorial: "Take twelve men from the people, from each tribe a man, and command them, saying, 'Take twelve stones from here out of the midst of the Jordan … and bring them with you, and lay them down in the place where you lodge tonight'" (4:2–3). Each tribe would carry a stone as a testimony of God's faithfulness. The act symbolized unity—twelve tribes, one miracle, one God.

Joshua obeyed immediately. The twelve men lifted the stones from where the priests' feet had stood, representing the moment when God's power had held back the waters. The stones were taken to their camp at Gilgal. Joshua also set up another pile of stones in the middle of the Jordan itself (4:9), perhaps marking the exact place where the priests had stood. Both memorials served as tangible witnesses of what God had done.

These stones were not mere decoration; they were declarations. In future generations, when children asked, "What do these stones mean to you?" (4:6), parents were to recount how "the waters of the Jordan were cut off before the ark of the covenant of the Lord" (4:7). Memory would sustain faith. The visible reminder of God's past faithfulness would inspire future obedience.

The people exalt God and Joshua (4:10-24)

When all the people had crossed safely, the priests remained standing until Joshua received the Lord's command to come up from the riverbed. As soon as the soles of their feet touched dry ground, "the waters of the Jordan returned to their place and overflowed all its banks, as before" (4:18). The timing again underscores divine control—nature obeyed the word of the Lord.

The Israelites encamped at Gilgal on the eastern border of Jericho, where Joshua set up the twelve stones (4:19-20). Gilgal would become a base of operations for the conquest and a place of renewal for Israel's covenant relationship with God. Joshua declared that the memorial was for future generations to remember "that the hand of the Lord is mighty, that you may fear the Lord your God forever" (4:24).

The people's reaction was reverent awe: "On that day the Lord exalted Joshua in the sight of all Israel, and they stood in awe of him just as they had stood in awe of Moses" (4:14). God's endorsement of Joshua's leadership united the nation under one purpose. The miracle at the Jordan was not just about geography—it was about authority and faith. The God who had been with Moses was now visibly with Joshua.

This crossing also had deep spiritual symbolism. The river marked the boundary between wilderness wandering and life in the promised land. Passing through the waters was a transition from old to new, from promise to fulfillment. In the New Testament, baptism echoes this same movement—from death to life, from slavery to salvation (Rom. 6:3-4). As Israel entered Canaan through faith and obedience, so Christians enter new life in Christ through faith expressed in obedience to the gospel.

The memorial stones at Gilgal further teach that faith must remember. Forgetfulness breeds disobedience, but remembrance fuels devotion. Each stone was a sermon in rock, declaring that the Lord of all the earth keeps his promises. Just as Israel's children would ask about the stones, so the church must continually retell the story of God's salvation—at the Lord's table, in worship, and in daily life.

The chapter closes with two lasting truths. First, God's power is not limited by natural barriers. Flooded rivers, fortified cities, and human weakness all yield to his command. Second, every generation must learn to trust and fear the Lord anew. The stones of Gilgal called Israel to remember that the same God who brought them through the river would fight their battles ahead.

APPLICATION

1. Faith moves forward

Israel's experience at the Jordan teaches that God's power is revealed when faith moves forward. The priests stood before a raging river at flood stage, yet the waters parted only after their feet touched the water's edge. God does not promise to remove every obstacle before we obey; he acts as we trust him enough to take the next step. Many believers today hesitate at the edge of obedience—afraid to forgive, to serve, or to surrender fully—waiting for certainty before they move. Yet faith is not waiting for proof; it is stepping out because God's promise is sure. Every act of faithful obedience becomes an invitation for God to display his strength. When we move forward in faith, he makes a way where there was none.

2. Keep your eyes on God's presence

Israel's success depended on keeping their eyes on the ark, the visible symbol of God's presence. The officers told the people, "Then you shall set out from your place and follow it." They were not to rush ahead or lag behind but to move in step with the Lord. Christians must learn that same discipline. When life's floods rise, the only safe course is to fix our attention on God's presence rather than on fear or self-reliance. We follow him by immersing ourselves in Scripture, by prayer, and by worshiping together as his people. When our focus drifts to our own strength, confusion and anxiety take over. But when our gaze rests on the Lord who leads us, he gives both direction and peace. His presence goes before us and makes every crossing possible.

3. Remember what God has done

The twelve stones taken from the Jordan served as more than decoration; they were declarations of God's power and faithfulness. Generations yet unborn would see those stones and ask, "What do these mean?"—and the story would be told again. Remembering nourishes faith. Christians need memorials too, not of stone but of gratitude. When we recount the ways

God has blessed, forgiven, and delivered us, our hearts are strengthened for future challenges. The Lord's Supper, songs of praise, and testimonies of answered prayer all remind us of the God who still works wonders. Forgetfulness weakens trust, but gratitude guards against fear. Faith grows best in the soil of remembrance.

4. Holiness before victory

Before Israel could see the waters part, Joshua said, "Consecrate yourselves, for tomorrow the Lord will do wonders among you." God's wonders are not performed for the careless or the indifferent but for those who prepare their hearts in holiness. Israel was not called to earn God's power but to honor his presence. Christians also must seek purity before progress. True victory—whether over temptation, bitterness, or apathy—comes when we surrender to God's sanctifying will. The call to holiness is not restrictive; it is redemptive. It frees us to walk boldly with the Lord who fights for us. Every great movement of God begins with a consecrated heart ready for obedience.

CONCLUSION

The crossing of the Jordan stands as one of Scripture's clearest pictures of obedient faith. The river did not part because Israel possessed strength or strategy but because they trusted the Lord enough to take the first step. God's presence, carried by the ark, went before them, and his power made a dry path through the flood. The stones at Gilgal became lasting reminders that the same God who delivers also deserves devotion. For Christians, the story calls us to remember God's past faithfulness, pursue holiness before him, and walk forward in confidence. When faith meets obedience, God always provides a way. The Jordan will part, the path will open, and his promises will prove true.

REFLECTION

1. What "Jordan River" moments have tested your faith and obedience?
2. How does God's timing in Joshua 3 challenge your patience and trust?
3. Why is consecration necessary before we see God's power at work?
4. What helps you keep your eyes on God's presence in uncertain times?
5. How can remembering God's past works strengthen your faith today?
6. Which of the twelve stones lessons do you most need to apply?

DISCUSSION

1. Why did God choose to perform another water miracle like the Red Sea crossing?
2. What does the ark's central role teach about God's presence and leadership?
3. How does this event foreshadow the salvation we receive through baptism?
4. Why is it important for believers to build "memorials" of God's faithfulness?
5. What does Joshua 3–4 reveal about leadership that depends on God?
6. How can the church today help one another take steps of faith together?

4

PREPARING FOR BATTLE
JOSHUA 5

Objective: To show that God's people must be consecrated and submissive before experiencing victory.

INTRODUCTION

The D-Day invasion of Normandy during World War II determined the future of Europe, but before they ever faced the beaches of France, Allied commanders paused the army. They reviewed strategy, repaired equipment, and reinforced morale. The soldiers longed for action, but their leaders knew that victory required more than numbers and weapons—it demanded readiness.

Joshua faced a similar moment on the plains of Jericho. Israel had just crossed the Jordan; the enemy trembled in fear. From a military standpoint, it was the perfect time to attack. Yet instead of advancing, God ordered the nation to stop. The men were circumcised, the Passover was celebrated, and the people consecrated themselves anew. Only then did Joshua meet the commander of the Lord's army. Before Israel could fight, they had to be made holy.

Joshua 5 teaches that spiritual victory always begins with spiritual preparation. God's people must be renewed in covenant, strengthened by remembrance, and humbled in submission before they can stand strong in battle. The Lord's greatest triumphs come not through strategy or strength but through hearts fully devoted to him.

EXAMINATION

The fear of the nations (5:1)

When the waters of the Jordan parted, word spread quickly through Canaan. "As soon as all the kings of the Amorites who were beyond the Jordan to the west, and all the kings of the Canaanites who were by the sea, heard that the Lord had dried up the waters of the Jordan for the people of Israel until they had crossed over, their hearts melted and there was no longer any spirit in them because of the people of Israel" (5:1). The terror Rahab had described (2:9–11) now gripped every ruler in the land. God had already begun softening the hearts of Israel's enemies.

Yet instead of pressing the advantage, Joshua paused. The logical move would have been to strike Jericho immediately while fear still paralyzed the Canaanites. But God's people were not ready for battle until they renewed their covenant. Before conquering others, they had to submit themselves. The Lord's victories come not through military strength but through spiritual preparation.

Renewing the covenant through circumcision (5:2–9)

At God's command, Joshua ordered the people to renew the covenant sign of circumcision. "At that time the Lord said to Joshua, 'Make flint knives and circumcise the sons of Israel a second time'" (5:2). The text explains, "All the people who came out of Egypt ... had been circumcised. Yet all the people who were born on the way in the wilderness ... had not been circumcised" (5:4–5). The new generation that had grown up in the desert had never received the sign of belonging to God's covenant.

This act was physically painful and strategically dangerous. The men would be incapacitated for several days—hardly the time to face an enemy city nearby. But faith always involves trust in God's protection. Israel had to choose between military prudence and covenant obedience. They chose obedience. The command to circumcise recalled God's covenant with Abraham (Gen. 17:9–14) and reaffirmed their identity as his chosen people.

The place where this occurred was named Gibeath-haaraloth, meaning "the hill of foreskins," and the camp itself was called Gilgal, meaning "rolling." The Lord said, "Today I have rolled away the reproach of Egypt from you" (5:9). This "reproach" likely referred to Israel's shame of slavery and wilderness wandering—the stigma of being a people who had left Egypt but never entered their inheritance. With this act, the Lord symbolically removed that disgrace. Circumcision marked them as his covenant nation, ready to claim his promises.

Spiritually, the same principle applies to believers under the new covenant. Paul describes Christian circumcision as a "circumcision made without hands"—the putting off of the old self in baptism (Col. 2:11–12). Just as Israel could not enter the promised land without covenant renewal, no one today enters the blessings of Christ without submitting to God's covenant terms in baptism. Obedience is the doorway to victory.

Celebrating the Passover (5:10–12)

After renewing the covenant sign, Israel observed the covenant meal. "While the people of Israel were encamped at Gilgal, they kept the Passover on the fourteenth day of the month in the evening on the plains of Jericho" (5:10). This was the first Passover in the land of promise, and it connected the nation's past deliverance with its present mission. The God who had redeemed them from Egypt would now give them victory in Canaan.

The timing is significant. The people celebrated Passover on the same date established in Exodus 12, demonstrating continuity between generations. Though the wilderness had delayed them, God's promises had not changed. They were still his redeemed people, dependent on his grace.

The next day, "they ate of the produce of the land, unleavened cakes and parched grain" (5:11). The manna that had sustained them for forty years stopped: "The manna ceased the day after they ate of the produce of the land. And there was no longer manna for the people of Israel, but they ate of the fruit of the land of Canaan that year" (5:12).

This transition marked a new era. God's miraculous provision gave way to ordinary blessings. They would now live by the fruit of the land rather than daily bread from heaven. The end of manna was not the end of grace; it was the beginning of maturity. God's people would still depend on him, but in a new way. He had brought them from survival to stewardship.

The commander of the Lord's army (5:13–15)

As Joshua surveyed Jericho, perhaps seeking strategy for the coming battle, he encountered a mysterious figure: "When Joshua was by Jericho, he lifted up his eyes and looked, and behold, a man was standing before him with his drawn sword in his hand" (5:13). Joshua approached boldly and asked, "Are you for us, or for our adversaries?" The man replied, "No; but I am the commander of the army of the Lord. Now I have come."

This was no ordinary soldier. Joshua fell on his face in reverence and said, "What does my lord say to his servant?" The commander answered, "Take off your sandals from your feet, for the place where you are standing is holy." The language mirrors Moses' encounter with God at the burning bush (Exod. 3:5), indicating that Joshua was in the presence of the divine. Many interpreters understand this "commander of the Lord's army" as a pre-incarnate appearance of Christ—the same "angel of the Lord" who represented God's authority and presence throughout the Old Testament (Exod. 23:20–23; Judg. 6:11–24).

The title "commander of the Lord's army" reveals a profound truth: the coming battle belonged to God, not Joshua. The Lord was not joining Israel's side; Israel was joining his. Victory in Canaan would not depend on human skill but on divine power. Joshua learned that leadership in God's kingdom begins with submission. Before he could lead Israel into battle, he had to bow before the true commander.

This moment reframed everything. The conquest was not a human campaign but a holy war waged by God himself against wickedness. Israel's task was not to seek divine support for their plans but to align themselves with God's. The drawn sword symbolized both judgment and deliverance—judgment on Canaan's corruption and deliverance for God's people.

Theological reflections

Joshua 5 marks a crucial turning point between preparation and conquest. Before Jericho's walls could fall, Israel had to be made ready in heart. Each episode of the chapter—circumcision, Passover, the end of manna, and Joshua's encounter—points to vital truths about faith and holiness.

First, *God's people must be consecrated before they can be victorious*. Obedience to God's covenant always precedes success in God's mission. Israel's delay for circumcision seemed illogical by human standards, but it demonstrated trust in divine protection. Similarly, the church must value purity above progress. Spiritual victories come to those who are wholly devoted to the Lord.

Second, *the Passover linked redemption to inheritance.* The same God who saved Israel from Egypt now sustained them in Canaan. Salvation is not the end of the journey but the beginning of service. Believers today commemorate their redemption through the Lord's Supper, remembering that the Lamb who was slain still leads his people to victory.

Third, *God provides for every stage of our journey.* The manna ceased when the people could eat the produce of the land. God's provision changes form but never ceases. Christians may experience seasons when divine provision seems sparse and responsibilities greater, but even then, God's faithfulness remains constant. He equips his people to live by faith in ordinary as well as extraordinary ways.

Finally, *the commander of the Lord's army reminds us who truly fights for us.* Joshua's encounter reveals that the battle belongs to the Lord. Our role is not to recruit God for our cause but to submit to his. Every Christian, like Joshua, must learn to remove their sandals before divine authority. Victory begins on holy ground—in humble worship and obedient surrender.

APPLICATION

1. Renew your covenant with God

Before facing Jericho, Israel paused for circumcision. It was a painful act of obedience that renewed their covenant identity. They could not fight the Lord's battles while living outside his will. Christians today face the same call to renewal. Faithfulness demands that we examine our hearts, repent of sin, and reaffirm our commitment to God. The victories we long for—in purity, perseverance, or ministry—flow from covenant loyalty. We cannot claim the promises of God while ignoring the responsibilities of his covenant. Every act of repentance renews our allegiance to the Lord who fights for us. Before the walls of our own challenges can fall, the heart must first be made holy.

2. Celebrate redemption regularly

Israel's first Passover in the land reminded them that the same God who delivered them from Egypt was still with them in Canaan. Remembering redemption deepened their gratitude and strengthened their faith for the battles ahead. Christians are called to that same rhythm of remembrance. Each time we partake of the Lord's Supper, we recall the Lamb who was slain and the salvation he secured. This weekly memorial is not a ritual of habit but an anchor of faith. When we look back to the cross, we find strength for present trials. Worship keeps our focus on the Redeemer rather than the difficulty. Victory begins at the table of remembrance.

3. Trust God's changing provision

When Israel entered the land, the manna stopped and they began eating the fruit of Canaan. God's provision changed, but his care did not. The Lord still sustained them, just in a new way. Christians often struggle when familiar blessings end or routines shift. Yet spiritual maturity means trusting God's faithfulness even when his methods differ. The end of one provision is not the absence of his presence. God calls us to rely on him daily, whether through other-worldly help or ordinary means. His grace adapts to each season of life, teaching us to depend on the Giver, not the gift.

4. Submit to the true commander

When Joshua met the commander of the Lord's army, he learned that victory was not about whose side God was on but about whether Israel was on God's side. Every believer must face that same realization. We do not ask God to bless our plans; we bow before his authority and align with his will. Christ, our commander, leads the battle against sin and darkness, and we follow his orders through humble obedience. Worship always precedes warfare. Before we can conquer, we must kneel. Every triumph begins when we take off our sandals and recognize that the battle belongs to the Lord.

CONCLUSION

Joshua 5 reminds us that holiness precedes victory. Before Israel could march around Jericho, they had to renew their covenant, celebrate redemption, and bow before the commander of the Lord's army. God delayed battle to prepare hearts. The same principle governs the Christian life—God works through a consecrated people, not a complacent one. He calls believers to renewal, remembrance, and reverence before conquest. True strength comes from submission; true readiness begins in worship. When we stand barefoot on holy ground, acknowledging that the battle belongs to the Lord, we are finally prepared to move forward in faith. Only the consecrated can become courageous, and only the humble can be made strong.

REFLECTION

1. Why did God delay Israel's attack to focus on renewal?
2. How does circumcision at Gilgal symbolize spiritual preparation today?
3. What does the Passover teach about remembering redemption before battle?
4. How do you respond when God's provision changes form but not faithfulness?
5. Why was Joshua's encounter with the commander essential before Jericho?
6. Where might God be calling you to remove your sandals in submission?

DISCUSSION

1. What risks did Israel face by obeying God's command to be circumcised near Jericho?
2. How does the end of manna demonstrate God's ongoing faithfulness in new ways?
3. Why must holiness come before effectiveness in God's mission?
4. How does the Lord's Supper parallel Israel's Passover at Gilgal?
5. What lessons about leadership does Joshua's humility before the commander reveal?
6. How can the church prepare spiritually before engaging in the Lord's battles today?

5

THE FALL OF JERICHO
JOSHUA 6

Objective: To show that faith and obedience bring victory because the battle belongs to the Lord.

INTRODUCTION

In 1989, the Berlin Wall—once considered impenetrable—crumbled almost overnight. For decades it had symbolized division, oppression, and fear. Governments had built it to last, but when people began to act in courage and faith, the wall that divided a continent came crashing down. What had stood for thirty years disappeared in a single moment, leaving behind freedom where barriers once stood.

Jericho's walls were even more formidable. They represented centuries of defiance against God and a human attempt to resist his purpose. When Israel arrived, the city was fortified and its gates locked tight. Yet the Lord told Joshua, "See, I have given Jericho into your hand." No army could breach those walls, but God's power would make them crumble. The victory would come not through weapons or strategy but through faith and obedience.

Joshua 6 is not merely about the fall of a city—it is about the triumph of faith. The walls of Jericho symbolize every obstacle that seems immovable, every challenge that tests our trust in God. When his people follow his commands, even when they seem illogical, he proves faithful. The same God who brought down Jericho's walls still tears down the strongholds that stand against his will.

EXAMINATION

God's plan for victory (6:1-5)

The city of Jericho stood as the first obstacle to Israel's conquest of Canaan. "Now Jericho was shut up inside and outside because of the people of Israel. None went out, and none came in" (6:1). The citizens of Jericho, terrified by the recent crossing of the Jordan, had sealed themselves within the city's massive walls. Humanly speaking, the situation was impossible—no siege weapons, no ladders, no experience. Yet the Lord declared, "See, I have given Jericho into your hand, with its king and mighty men of valor" (6:2). The victory was promised before the battle began.

God then revealed his unusual strategy. "You shall march around the city, all the men of war going around the city once. Thus shall you do for six days. Seven priests shall bear seven trumpets of rams' horns before the ark. On the seventh day you shall march around the city seven times, and the priests shall blow the trumpets" (6:3-4). When they heard the long blast of the horn, the people were to shout, and the wall would fall flat (6:5).

The plan defied logic. No weapon or human ingenuity could bring down Jericho's walls. God's purpose was to teach Israel that victory depends on obedience, not power. The ark's central place in the procession reminded the people that the Lord himself fought for them. Seven priests, seven trumpets, and seven days emphasized divine completeness. The battle would be won through faith expressed in action—a lesson later echoed in Hebrews 11:30: "By faith the walls of Jericho fell down after they had been encircled for seven days."

Archaeological excavations at ancient Jericho have revealed remains consistent with the biblical account of a fortified city. John Garstang's 1930s dig uncovered a double wall system—an outer stone retaining wall topped with mudbrick and a second mudbrick wall above it, both more than six feet thick—showing evidence of sudden collapse and a fiery destruction dated around 1400 BC, matching the traditional date for Joshua's conquest. Kathleen Kenyon's later excavations re-dated the destruction to centuries earlier, arguing Jericho was unfortified in Joshua's time. However, Bryant Wood's reevaluation in the 1990s challenged her conclusions, citing pottery and carbon data supporting Garstang's earlier dating. While debate continues, the evidence points to a heavily fortified city that suffered a catastrophic fall in the Late Bronze Age—remarkably consistent with the biblical record in Joshua 6.

Israel obeys God's command (6:6–14)

Joshua relayed the Lord's instructions to the priests and people. "Take up the ark of the covenant, and let seven priests bear seven trumpets of rams' horns before the ark of the Lord" (6:6). The army advanced, the priests blew the trumpets, and the ark followed, but Joshua commanded silence: "You shall not shout or make your voice heard … until the day I tell you to shout" (6:10). For six days, the nation marched once around the city in silence.

The scene must have appeared foolish to Jericho's defenders—thousands circling their walls, trumpets sounding, but no attack. Yet each silent march was a statement of faith. Obedience requires patience and perseverance, even when we do not understand God's timing. Israel learned to wait on the Lord's command. The priests blowing the trumpets each day reminded the people that this was no military campaign; it was a sacred procession led by the presence of God.

For six days, nothing seemed to happen. The walls still stood; Jericho's gates remained closed. But unseen, God was working. Faith often requires repetitive obedience in the face of apparent inaction. Israel's silence and steady marching prepared them for the moment when God would act.

The fall of Jericho (6:15–21)

"On the seventh day they rose early, at the dawn of day, and marched around the city in the same manner seven times. It was only on that day that they marched around the city seven times" (6:15). On the seventh circuit, Joshua commanded, "Shout, for the Lord has given you the city" (6:16). The priests blew the trumpets, the people shouted, and "the wall fell down flat, so that the people went up into the city … and they captured the city" (6:20).

The collapse of Jericho's walls was supernatural. Archaeological studies have confirmed that Jericho's ancient walls did indeed fall outward—an unlikely direction for a siege. Scripture leaves no doubt: God caused the walls to fall. The timing of their obedience and God's action was perfect. When the people acted in faith, God acted in power.

Joshua also declared that Jericho was "devoted to the Lord for destruction" (6:17). The Hebrew term *herem* signified something set apart to God, either for sacred use or for complete destruction. Everything in Jericho belonged to God. The gold, silver, bronze, and iron were to be placed in the Lord's treasury (6:19, 24), but all other property and inhabitants were to be destroyed. The command was severe but just. Canaan's corruption had reached its limit (Gen. 15:16). This was not cruelty but divine judgment executed through Israel as God's instrument.

Amid judgment, however, mercy appeared. "But Rahab the prostitute and her father's household and all who belonged to her, Joshua saved alive" (6:25). The scarlet cord she had displayed in faith (2:21) marked her house for salvation. Thus, the walls fell for everyone except those who trusted the Lord's promise. Grace stood side by side with judgment, illustrating God's consistent nature—justice against sin, mercy toward faith.

The curse on Jericho (6:22-27)

After Rahab and her family were brought out and settled near Israel's camp, Joshua issued a solemn warning: "Cursed before the Lord be the man who rises up and rebuilds this city, Jericho. At the cost of his firstborn shall he lay its foundation, and at the cost of his youngest son shall he set up its gates" (6:26). Jericho was to remain a permanent reminder that victory belongs to the Lord. The curse symbolized finality—Jericho would never again stand in defiance of God. Centuries later, during Ahab's reign, this curse was fulfilled when Hiel of Bethel rebuilt Jericho and lost both his sons (1 Kgs. 16:34).

The chapter ends with divine approval: "So the Lord was with Joshua, and his fame was in all the land" (6:27). God's presence validated Joshua's leadership and Israel's faith. Their obedience brought victory, their faith brought glory to God, and their restraint preserved holiness.

Theological reflections

Jericho's fall teaches timeless truths about faith, obedience, and divine power. First, *victory begins with faith in God's promises*. Israel did not conquer

Jericho through strength but through trust. God declared, "I have given Jericho into your hand" before a single step was taken. Faith accepts God's word as certain even when circumstances appear impossible.

Second, *obedience, even when it seems illogical, is the key to success*. Marching in circles for a week must have seemed absurd, yet God uses such commands to test our submission. The Lord's ways often defy human reasoning so that his glory becomes unmistakable.

Third, *God's judgment is righteous and his mercy real*. Jericho's destruction fulfilled divine justice against sin that had persisted for generations. Yet within that judgment, Rahab and her family found salvation through faith. The same God who judges also redeems.

Fourth, *the victory belongs entirely to God*. The walls fell by his power, not human effort. Faith did not cause the walls to fall; God did, in response to obedient faith. In every age, salvation and victory come from the Lord, not from human merit or strength.

Finally, *Jericho stands as a warning and a witness*. It warns that defiance against God leads to ruin, yet it witnesses that faith in his promise leads to life. The same God who brought down Jericho's walls still calls his people to trust, obey, and remember that the battle is the Lord's.

APPLICATION

1. Faith trusts God's promises before they are fulfilled

When God told Joshua, "See, I have given Jericho into your hand," the walls were still standing, the gates were shut, and the enemy inside remained strong. Yet God spoke of victory as already accomplished. That is the nature of divine promise—it is certain before it is visible. For six days, Israel marched without seeing any result. Still, they obeyed, because faith believes what God has said even when the outcome seems impossible. Christians are called to the same kind of trust. We obey Scripture's commands—praying for our enemies, forgiving wrongs, persevering in service—before we see change, because we know the Lord keeps his word. Faith walks in circles around the walls of impossibility, confident that God's promises will stand. True faith moves forward, not because the evidence is clear, but because God is faithful.

2. Obedience, not understanding, brings victory

The plan God gave Joshua defied all logic. From a military perspective, marching silently around Jericho for a week was absurd. Yet Israel obeyed without hesitation. Their obedience revealed that they trusted God's wisdom more than their own. The Lord's instructions to his people today sometimes challenge our understanding as well. We may not grasp why baptism is essential or why forgiveness is commanded even for those who hurt us. But faith obeys because it knows God's wisdom surpasses human reasoning. Spiritual victories are never won by strategy or strength but by submission. The walls fall only when God's people act in faith. When we obey, even in the small details, the Lord turns what seems foolish to the world into displays of his glory.

3. God's mercy extends even in judgment

Amid the destruction of Jericho, one home stood untouched—the house of Rahab. The same God who brought down the city walls preserved the life of a woman who trusted in his promise. Her scarlet cord, like the blood on Israel's doorposts in Egypt, marked her household for salvation. The fall of Jericho reminds us that divine justice and divine mercy are never at odds. God hates sin, yet he always provides a refuge for the penitent. The gospel fulfills this truth completely. The blood of Christ is the scarlet cord that shields all who come to him in faith. Just as Rahab's obedience brought safety to her family, so our faith in Jesus brings salvation to all who believe. Even when judgment falls, the grace of God still shines, calling sinners to take refuge in his mercy.

4. The victory belongs to the Lord

When the people shouted and the walls collapsed, Israel could take no credit. They had marched, waited, and obeyed, but only God had the power to make stone crumble. Their triumph was not the result of human strength but of divine power working through faith. Every Christian battle—against temptation, fear, or discouragement—is won the same way. We fight, but the Lord gives victory. We obey, but he supplies the strength. The fall of Jericho warns us against pride and self-reliance. Success in the Lord's work must always point back to him. Our achievements, conversions, or answered prayers are not trophies of human skill but testimonies to God's faithfulness. The battle is his; the glory is his. When we give him credit for every victory, we remain humble and ready for whatever challenge lies ahead.

CONCLUSION

The fall of Jericho stands as one of the clearest demonstrations of God's power and faithfulness. The walls that seemed invincible collapsed at the sound of trumpets and the shout of obedient faith. Israel's victory was not earned through strength or strategy but received through trust in the Lord. Rahab's deliverance revealed that God's mercy still reaches those who believe, even in a world under judgment. For Christians, this story echoes the life of faith—we march, we wait, we obey, and God gives the victory. Whatever walls rise before us—fear, temptation, grief, or sin—the same God who brought down Jericho's defenses still fights for his people. The battle is his, and when we follow his word in faith, no wall can stand against him.

REFLECTION

1. What does Jericho's fall teach about trusting God's timing?
2. How can you demonstrate faith when God's plan seems illogical?
3. Which "walls" in your life require patient obedience to God's word?
4. How does Rahab's salvation reveal both God's justice and mercy?
5. What practices help you remember that victory belongs to the Lord?
6. Where is God calling you to step forward in faith this week?

DISCUSSION

1. Why did God choose such an unconventional plan to defeat Jericho?
2. How does the ark's role emphasize God's presence in the battle?
3. What lessons can believers learn from Israel's silent obedience?
4. How does Rahab's deliverance connect to salvation through Christ's blood?
5. Why is it dangerous to claim victory without giving glory to God?
6. How can the church today model Israel's unity and faith in God's promises?

6

SIN IN THE CAMP

JOSHUA 7

Objective: To remind students that hidden sin destroys fellowship and victory until it is confessed and removed.

INTRODUCTION

In 1986, the space shuttle Challenger exploded seventy-three seconds after liftoff, killing all seven astronauts aboard. The investigation later revealed that the cause was not a major design flaw or catastrophic engine failure but a small rubber O-ring that failed to seal in the cold. One overlooked weakness brought disaster to an entire mission. What seemed minor proved deadly.

Achan's sin in Joshua 7 carries the same lesson. After Jericho's triumph, Israel felt unstoppable. Yet one man's hidden disobedience led to national defeat. What Achan buried beneath his tent—silver, gold, and a beautiful cloak—brought shame, fear, and death upon the whole camp. The Lord's anger burned not because of the size of the sin but because of the breach of covenant faithfulness.

Joshua 7 reminds believers that no sin is too small to matter. The strength of God's people depends on holiness, not numbers or victories. Before Israel could rise again, they had to confront the corruption within.

The same is true for the church today. Hidden sin weakens our witness, grieves the Spirit, and blocks God's blessing. Only when sin is confessed and removed can God's power return to his people.

EXAMINATION

The hidden sin (7:1)

The triumph at Jericho quickly gave way to tragedy. The chapter opens with chilling contrast: "But the people of Israel broke faith in regard to the devoted things, for Achan ... took some of the devoted things. And the anger of the Lord burned against the people of Israel" (7:1). One man's sin affected the entire nation. The "devoted things" (*herem*) from Jericho had been set apart for destruction or for the Lord's treasury (6:18-19). To take them was to rob God himself.

The phrase "broke faith" implies betrayal. Israel had entered covenant with the Lord, yet Achan's theft violated that sacred bond. His sin was secret, but its consequences were public. Scripture consistently teaches that sin cannot remain hidden forever. What is concealed in private will eventually disrupt the fellowship of God's people. Achan's greed introduced rot into the heart of a holy nation.

Defeat at Ai (7:2-5)

Unaware of Achan's sin, Joshua sent spies to scout Ai, a small city near Bethel. The spies reported, "Do not have all the people go up, but let about two or three thousand men go up and attack Ai. Do not make the whole people toil up there, for they are few" (7:3). Confident from Jericho's victory, Israel relied on human assessment rather than divine direction. There is no record that Joshua consulted the Lord.

When three thousand men attacked, "they fled before the men of Ai, and the men of Ai killed about thirty-six of their men and chased them before the gate as far as Shebarim" (7:4-5). The defeat stunned Israel. Fear spread through the camp: "The hearts of the people melted and became as water." The same phrase once described Canaan's terror at Israel's approach (2:11; 5:1), but now God's people trembled instead. Sin had reversed the victory.

Their failure was not due to military weakness but moral compromise. The Lord's favor had departed because of disobedience. Success in spiritual battles depends not on numbers or strategy but on holiness. When sin is tolerated in God's people, defeat is inevitable.

Joshua's lament and God's response (7:6–15)

In grief and confusion, "Joshua tore his clothes and fell to the earth on his face before the ark of the Lord until the evening" (7:6). The elders joined him in mourning. Joshua cried out, "Alas, O Lord God, why have you brought this people over the Jordan at all, to give us into the hands of the Amorites, to destroy us?" (7:7). His words echo Israel's earlier complaints in the wilderness, but they sprang from despair rather than rebellion. Joshua could not understand why God's promise seemed broken.

God's reply was immediate and firm: "Get up! Why have you fallen on your face? Israel has sinned; they have transgressed my covenant that I commanded them" (7:10–11). The Lord made clear that the issue was not divine failure but human disobedience. "They have taken some of the devoted things; they have stolen and lied and put them among their own belongings." Because of this, "I will be with you no more, unless you destroy the devoted things from among you" (7:12).

The Lord commanded Joshua to sanctify the people and prepare for judgment: "You cannot stand before your enemies until you take away the devoted things from among you" (7:13). The next morning, God would expose the guilty party through a solemn process of selection—tribe by tribe, clan by clan, household by household—until the sinner was revealed (7:14–15). The Lord's justice would be thorough and righteous.

This scene highlights an essential principle: holiness must precede victory. Israel's failure at Ai was not due to weak soldiers but to defiled hearts. God's presence cannot abide with sin. Repentance, not strategy, was the nation's only hope.

Achan's confession and punishment (7:16–26)

Early the next morning, Joshua led Israel through the process of exposure. The tribe of Judah was taken, then the clan of the Zerahites, then the household of Zabdi, and finally Achan, Zabdi's grandson, was singled out (7:16–18). Each narrowing step increased the tension, reminding the nation that God sees what man cannot hide.

Joshua urged Achan, "My son, give glory to the Lord God of Israel and give praise to him. And tell me now what you have done; do not hide it from me" (7:19). Confession was not optional—it was the only way to restore peace in the community. Achan replied, "Truly I have sinned against the Lord God of Israel, and this is what I did: when I saw among the spoil a beautiful cloak from Shinar, and two hundred shekels of silver, and a bar of gold weighing fifty shekels, then I coveted them and took them" (7:20–21).

His words trace the tragic progression of sin: *I saw, I coveted, I took.* The same sequence appears in Genesis 3:6, when Eve saw the fruit, desired it, and ate. Sin begins with the eyes, takes root in the heart, and bears fruit in the hands. What Achan "saw" was beautiful but forbidden. What he "coveted" became a chain around his soul.

Messengers found the stolen items hidden in his tent and laid them out before the Lord (7:22–23). Nothing could be concealed from divine sight. Judgment followed: Achan, his family, and his possessions were taken to the Valley of Achor. There, Joshua declared, "Why did you bring trouble on us? The Lord brings trouble on you today" (7:25). The people stoned them, burned their remains, and raised a heap of stones as a warning. "Then the Lord turned from his burning anger" (7:26).

The punishment may seem harsh to modern readers, but it underscores the seriousness of sin in a holy community. Achan's entire household likely shared in his guilt by concealing the stolen items. Sin contaminates everything it touches. The Valley of Achor ("trouble") became a monument to divine justice—but later prophets would call it a place of hope (Hos. 2:15). Through repentance, even the valley of trouble can become a door of renewal.

Theological reflections

Joshua 7 confronts readers with the devastating consequences of sin among God's people. Its message is sobering but necessary.

First, *personal sin brings collective consequences.* Though only one man disobeyed, "the people of Israel broke faith." Achan's theft removed God's blessing from the entire nation. In the church, hidden sin can likewise weaken the body's integrity and effectiveness. Holiness is never private—it affects the whole community of faith (1 Cor. 5:6).

Second, *sin always separates us from God's presence*. The Lord told Joshua, "I will be with you no more, unless you destroy the devoted things from among you." Victory vanished when sin entered the camp. Until repentance and discipline restored purity, Israel could not stand before its enemies. The same truth holds for believers today: forgiveness requires confession, and fellowship requires holiness (1 John 1:7–9).

Third, *confession must lead to removal*. Achan's confession was genuine, but repentance demanded more than words. The stolen items had to be destroyed, and the sin completely removed from the camp. True repentance exposes sin to the light and eliminates it from one's life. God's people cannot expect renewal while cherishing what he has condemned.

Fourth, *God's judgment reveals his holiness but also prepares the way for grace*. The valley that symbolized Achan's downfall later became a picture of restoration (Hos. 2:15). Judgment is never God's final word; mercy waits on the other side of repentance.

Finally, Joshua 7 teaches that *obedience and holiness are inseparable from victory*. Israel would never conquer Canaan through numbers or strategy, but only through faith and purity. The same is true for the church today. The Lord still calls his people to cleanse their hearts, remove hidden sin, and walk in holiness before him. Only then can his power rest upon them.

APPLICATION

1. Hidden sin weakens the whole body

Achan's secret theft brought defeat to the entire nation. What one man hid in his tent disrupted God's blessing on millions. Scripture repeatedly warns that sin is never private; it poisons relationships, undermines fellowship, and drives away God's presence. In the church, hidden sin can cripple effectiveness and destroy unity. When believers tolerate what God condemns—dishonesty, impurity, bitterness, or pride—they invite weakness into the body of Christ. The lesson is clear: holiness is not optional but essential. Every Christian shares responsibility for maintaining purity within the Lord's people. When sin remains unconfessed, victory turns to defeat; but when repentance comes, God's favor returns. We must examine our own "tents" and remove whatever defiles, knowing that the strength of God's people depends on the holiness of each heart.

2. Disobedience replaces confidence with fear

Israel approached Ai with self-assurance, assuming the victory would be as effortless as Jericho. Yet hidden sin had severed their connection with God's power. When the battle began, they fled in fear. Spiritual confidence cannot survive disobedience. Christians lose courage when sin reigns unchallenged, because the conscience knows what the lips deny. Disobedience drains strength, silences prayer, and breeds defeat. The fear that once belonged to the enemy now falls upon God's people. The only cure is repentance and restoration. When the heart is cleansed and the will aligned with God's word, confidence returns—not in self, but in the Lord who forgives. The story of Ai warns believers that victory depends not on experience or reputation, but on continual obedience to God's commands.

3. True repentance requires exposure and removal

When Achan confessed, his words alone could not restore Israel. The stolen items had to be brought out and destroyed. Repentance always involves both confession and cleansing. Many try to hide sin under layers of denial, hoping time will erase it. But God's holiness demands exposure. What is buried must be brought into the light and removed. The same is true in our lives today. Confession without change is empty; remorse without repentance leaves the heart unchanged. Genuine repentance brings transformation—turning from sin to righteousness, from secrecy to surrender. The Lord will not dwell where sin is concealed, but he delights to forgive when it is confessed. The valley of trouble becomes a place of hope only when sin is uncovered and removed completely from our midst.

4. God's holiness demands accountability

The punishment of Achan may seem severe, but it demonstrates how seriously God regards sin among his people. His justice was not cruelty but covenant faithfulness. A holy God cannot ignore rebellion. The church must recover this reverence for God's holiness. Grace does not excuse disobedience; it empowers transformation. Christians must hold one another accountable in love, seeking restoration rather than punishment but never tolerating sin's presence. Discipline, confession, and repentance are all acts of mercy that guard the purity of Christ's body. The Lord's anger turned away only when sin was removed. Likewise, renewal in the church begins when we take God's holiness as seriously as he does. When we pursue righteousness together, his presence returns, and victory becomes possible once more.

CONCLUSION

The defeat at Ai revealed that sin in the camp is far more dangerous than enemies outside it. Israel's strength had never been in numbers, strategy, or courage—it was in the presence of a holy God. Achan's disobedience shattered that fellowship, and until the sin was exposed and removed, the nation could not stand. God still calls his people to the same seriousness about holiness. Hidden sin drains power, divides hearts, and quenches the Spirit. But when confession replaces concealment, grace restores what guilt has broken. The Valley of Achor became a place of judgment, yet later prophets called it a "door of hope." God's discipline still leads to mercy for those who repent. Victory always returns when sin is forsaken and holiness is renewed.

REFLECTION

1. What does Achan's story teach about the seriousness of "small" sins?
2. How can personal sin harm the spiritual strength of an entire congregation?
3. Why is confession necessary before renewal can begin?
4. What "hidden things" might be keeping you from victory?
5. How does Joshua 7 reveal both God's justice and his mercy?
6. What steps can you take to keep your heart pure before God?

DISCUSSION

1. Why did God hold the whole nation accountable for one man's sin?
2. What are the modern equivalents of "devoted things" that Christians must avoid?
3. How does Achan's confession show both guilt and grace?
4. Why must repentance include both confession and removal of sin?
5. How should the church practice loving accountability without becoming harsh?
6. How does the Valley of Achor become a "door of hope" for God's people today?

7

VICTORY AT AI

JOSHUA 8

Objective: To show that God restores victory and purpose when his people repent and obey his word.

INTRODUCTION

In 1958, a young baseball player named Bill Mazeroski made a critical mistake that cost his team a championship game. Reporters mocked him, and fans jeered, calling him unreliable. Yet two years later, that same player hit the walk-off home run that won the 1960 World Series for Pittsburgh. The one once remembered for failure became the symbol of victory. Sometimes the greatest triumphs are born from lessons learned in defeat.

Israel's story at Ai follows the same pattern. Chapter 7 ended with humiliation—defeat, confession, and judgment. But Joshua 8 opens with mercy. God's words, "Do not fear and do not be dismayed," reminded the people that failure is never final when repentance is real. Cleansed and renewed, they rose to face the same city that had shamed them before. This time, God gave them both strategy and strength.

The victory at Ai teaches that restoration begins when God's people return to obedience. Past mistakes need not define the future when grace renews the heart. Whether in ancient battlefields or modern lives, the same truth holds: when sin is confessed and faith restored, the Lord gives victory once more. Ai became a monument to what God can do with a repentant and obedient people.

EXAMINATION

Renewed assurance and divine strategy (8:1–2)

After the crushing defeat at Ai and the judgment on Achan, Israel stood humbled and fearful. But God's grace speaks even after failure. "And the Lord said to Joshua, 'Do not fear and do not be dismayed. Take all the fighting men with you, and arise, go up to Ai. See, I have given into your hand the king of Ai, and his people, his city, and his land'" (8:1). The same words that once announced victory over Jericho now reaffirmed it for Ai. God was restoring confidence to a repentant nation.

This time the Lord commanded a different approach: "Lay an ambush against the city, behind it" (8:2). At Jericho, victory had come through a miraculous collapse; at Ai, it would come through divine strategy. Both methods demonstrated that the Lord, not human might, secured success. God does not always repeat his miracles—he teaches his people to trust his guidance in new ways. Having confessed sin and renewed holiness, Israel was again ready to act under his direction.

The ambush is set (8:3–13)

Joshua immediately obeyed. He selected thirty thousand valiant warriors by night and sent them to lie in ambush behind the city (8:3–4). Their instructions were precise: "You shall rise up from the ambush and seize the city, for the Lord your God will give it into your hand" (8:7). Joshua emphasized that victory would again be the Lord's doing, not Israel's ingenuity.

The main army, led by Joshua himself, camped north of Ai, while another force of about five thousand men was stationed west of the city to complete the ambush (8:12). The stage was set for a two-pronged attack—one that would draw Ai's forces out and leave the city defenseless. Unlike the overconfident rush of chapter 7, this plan reflected careful obedience and dependence on God's word.

Israel's return to Ai was not merely a military operation; it was an act of faith. Having experienced defeat through sin, the people now moved forward in renewed trust. God often allows failure to refine faith, so that his people learn to follow his commands more closely the second time.

The battle and victory (8:14–23)

At dawn, the king of Ai saw Israel's army and hurried out to attack, unaware of the ambush waiting behind his city. Joshua and his men feigned retreat, drawing the enemy away from Ai just as the Lord had planned. "There was not a man left in Ai or Bethel who did not go out after Israel. They left the city open and pursued Israel" (8:17).

Then came the turning point: "The Lord said to Joshua, 'Stretch out the javelin that is in your hand toward Ai, for I will give it into your hand.' And Joshua stretched out the javelin toward the city" (8:18). This symbolic gesture, reminiscent of Moses lifting his staff over the Red Sea (Exod. 14:16), signified divine authority. As Joshua's hand was raised, the ambush force rose, entered the city, and set it on fire (8:19). When Ai's soldiers looked back and saw smoke rising, their courage collapsed. Israel turned back to face them, trapping the enemy between two forces. "And Israel struck them down, until there was left none that survived or escaped" (8:22).

The Lord fulfilled his promise completely. The defeat that had once humiliated Israel now became a testimony of restoration. God's people learned that failure is never final when they return to him in repentance and faith.

The destruction of Ai (8:24–29)

The battle ended with total victory. Israel killed twelve thousand people, the entire population of Ai (8:25). The king was captured alive and brought before Joshua. "But the livestock and the spoil of that city Israel took as their plunder, according to the word of the Lord that he commanded Joshua" (8:27). At Jericho, the spoils had been forbidden; at Ai, they were permitted. God was not inconsistent—he was teaching obedience. The issue had never been wealth but submission to his will. When Israel obeyed, God blessed them freely.

Joshua held his javelin stretched out until the battle was over, just as Moses had held up his hands during Israel's earlier victory over Amalek (Exod. 17:11–13). His raised weapon symbolized steadfast dependence on God's power. The city was burned and reduced to ruins. "The king of Ai he hanged on a tree until evening. And at sunset Joshua commanded, and they took his body down from the tree and threw it at the entrance of the gate of the city and raised over it a great heap of stones" (8:29). The pile of stones served as a perpetual reminder of the consequences of rebellion and the faithfulness of divine justice.

Through obedience, Israel transformed a site of shame into a monument of victory. Where sin had brought defeat, repentance and faith brought triumph.

Renewal of covenant worship (8:30–35)

After the battle, Joshua led the people north to Mount Ebal, near Shechem, to renew their covenant with God. This act was not an afterthought but a direct fulfillment of Moses' command in Deuteronomy 27. "At that time Joshua built an altar to the Lord, the God of Israel, on Mount Ebal" (8:30). The altar was made of uncut stones, according to the law, symbolizing purity and reverence. Burnt offerings and peace offerings were presented, expressing both atonement and gratitude (8:31).

Joshua then wrote a copy of the law on the stones and read it aloud before all Israel—"the sojourner as well as the native born" (8:33-35). Half the tribes stood on Mount Gerizim for blessing, the other half on Mount Ebal for cursing, as Moses had prescribed. The scene was profoundly communal and covenantal: men, women, children, and foreigners all heard the word of the Lord.

This ceremony confirmed that Israel's success depended on obedience to Scripture, not military strength. The nation had learned that spiritual renewal, not victory, was their greatest need. Only when God's people live by his revealed word can they enjoy his abiding presence and peace.

Theological reflections

Joshua 8 reveals how repentance restores both relationship and purpose. It begins where Joshua 7 left off—with sin judged, fellowship restored, and God once again leading his people.

First, *God offers renewal after repentance.* The same God who disciplined Israel now encouraged them, saying, "Do not fear." Divine correction is never meant to destroy but to restore. When sin is confessed and removed, grace revives confidence for renewed obedience.

Second, ***victory comes through divine direction.*** The Lord's strategy for Ai contrasted sharply with Jericho's. Sometimes God works through miracles; other times through means. Either way, success depends on obedience to his word. Christians must seek his guidance afresh rather than relying on past experiences or formulas.

Third, ***obedience restores blessing.*** At Jericho, Israel's disobedience brought loss; at Ai, obedience brought abundance. The permission to keep the spoils underscored that God delights to bless those who follow his instructions faithfully.

Fourth, ***worship anchors every victory.*** The covenant renewal at Mount Ebal demonstrated that the ultimate goal was not conquest but communion with God. Victories are hollow without worship. Israel's renewed altar proclaimed that glory belongs to the Lord alone.

Finally, ***failure does not have to define God's people.*** Through repentance and renewed faith, Israel turned the place of defeat into a place of triumph. For believers today, the same truth holds: our past failures need not determine our future faithfulness. When we return to God, he restores both our purpose and our peace.

APPLICATION

1. Failure is not final when repentance is real

Israel's first attempt at Ai ended in shame because of hidden sin, but repentance opened the door to restoration. God's first words after their defeat were, "Do not fear and do not be dismayed." The Lord delights to give new beginnings to the humble. Many Christians live under the weight of past mistakes, convinced they have forfeited God's favor forever. Yet Joshua 8 proves that grace still meets those who return with contrite hearts. Forgiveness restores confidence, and obedience restores purpose. The same God who disciplined Israel also led them back into battle. Christians must learn to leave the valley of failure and rise in faith, knowing that repentance is not the end—it is the beginning of renewal. When sin is confessed and forsaken, God redeems even our defeats for his glory.

2. God's methods may change, but his faithfulness never does

At Jericho, the walls fell by miracle; at Ai, victory came by strategy. The difference teaches us that God's power is not limited to one method. He sometimes acts through the extraordinary and sometimes through the ordinary, but he remains the same faithful Lord. Christians must resist the temptation to rely on yesterday's experiences or formulas. What worked before may not be what God desires now. He calls his people to trust his presence, not our patterns. Whether through unexpected miracles or quiet perseverance, victory comes when we follow his word. God's diverse methods remind us that he is not predictable, but he is always trustworthy. His wisdom fits each battle perfectly, shaping us to depend not on habit or history, but on his living guidance every day.

3. Obedience brings blessing and renewed confidence

The difference between defeat in Joshua 7 and victory in Joshua 8 was not in Israel's strength but in their obedience. At Jericho, disobedience brought loss; at Ai, obedience brought success. The same truth applies to every believer. When we align our actions with God's will, his favor returns, and our confidence grows—not in ourselves, but in him. Notice that God allowed Israel to keep the spoils of Ai, teaching that he withholds no good thing from those who walk uprightly. Our task is to obey; his role is to bless. The path of obedience may not always be easy, but it is always fruitful. Each step of faith restores courage and renews joy in the Lord. Obedience is not the means to earn grace; it is the evidence that grace has truly changed our hearts.

4. Worship must follow every victory

After the triumph at Ai, Joshua did not celebrate with a military parade—he built an altar. Israel's greatest act of victory was not the conquest of a city but the renewal of their covenant with God. True success leads to worship, not pride. Christians today must learn this rhythm: after every answered prayer, every breakthrough, every success, we return to the altar in gratitude. Worship keeps victory from turning into vanity. It reminds us that all blessings come from the Lord and belong to him. When we give God the glory, our hearts stay humble and our fellowship stays strong. The mountain of worship must always follow the battlefield of obedience. Every triumph should end, as Israel's did, in renewed devotion to the One who made it possible.

CONCLUSION

Joshua 8 stands as a testimony that grace can turn failure into triumph. The same nation that once fled in fear now conquered in faith, not because their strength had grown but because their hearts had changed. God's command, "Do not fear and do not be dismayed," reminded Israel—and reminds us—that the Lord is willing to begin again with the repentant. The spoils of Ai replaced the shame of Achan; worship on Mount Ebal replaced the sorrow of defeat. When God's people return to obedience, he renews both courage and blessing. The story of Ai assures believers that sin's consequences are not the end of the story. In Christ, forgiveness leads to restoration, and faith leads again to victory. The God who forgives failure still grants fresh beginnings to those who trust and obey.

REFLECTION

1. What does God's encouragement in verse 1 reveal about his grace after failure?
2. Why was repentance necessary before Israel could experience victory again?
3. How does Ai's defeat and restoration mirror your own walk of faith?
4. What does Joshua's raised javelin teach about dependence on God's power?
5. Why must worship follow every victory in the Christian life?
6. How can you turn past failures into testimonies of God's faithfulness?

DISCUSSION

1. Why did God choose a different battle plan for Ai than for Jericho?
2. How does this story show the balance between divine power and human effort?
3. What lessons can the church learn from Israel's renewal of covenant worship?
4. Why is it important to seek God's guidance before acting, even after success?
5. How does Israel's obedience at Ai demonstrate true repentance?
6. What practices help believers keep their confidence rooted in God, not themselves?

8

THE GIBEONITE DECEPTION
JOSHUA 9

Objective: To affirm that Christians must seek God's counsel, keep their word, and trust his mercy to redeem mistakes.

INTRODUCTION

In 1872, an Englishman named George Psalmanazar became famous for claiming to be a native of Formosa (modern-day Taiwan). He spoke a made-up language, invented an alphabet, and fabricated an entire culture. Scholars and church leaders praised him as an expert—until the truth emerged. Psalmanazar had deceived an empire. His story became a lasting warning: appearances can mislead even the wise when truth is not tested carefully.

Joshua faced a similar deception in the land of Canaan. After Jericho and Ai, Israel's reputation spread throughout the region. Most kings united to fight, but the Gibeonites took another path. Pretending to be travelers from a distant land, they approached Joshua seeking peace. Their plan succeeded—not because they were clever, but because Joshua and the leaders "did not ask counsel from the Lord."

The Gibeonite deception teaches that spiritual discernment cannot rely on appearances alone. Even faithful people can make foolish decisions when prayer is neglected. Yet the chapter also reveals God's mercy. Though deceived, Joshua honored his oath, and the Lord redeemed the outcome for good. The Gibeonites were spared, the covenant was upheld, and God's faithfulness remained unbroken. From this episode, Christians learn to seek divine wisdom, speak truthfully, and trust that God's grace can redeem even our mistakes.

EXAMINATION

The nations unite against Israel (9:1-2)

Word of Israel's victories spread rapidly through Canaan. "As soon as all the kings who were beyond the Jordan in the hill country and in the lowland … heard of this, they gathered together as one to fight against Joshua and Israel" (9:1-2). The miraculous fall of Jericho and Ai left no doubt that the Lord fought for his people. The Canaanites' reaction, however, was not repentance but resistance. Rather than submit to the God of heaven, they chose rebellion. This alliance represented humanity's age-old defiance of God's purposes—nations uniting not in faith but in opposition to his will.

Among the Canaanites, one group took a different approach. The inhabitants of Gibeon, a city about six miles northwest of Jerusalem, realized that open warfare against Israel was futile. They had heard what the Lord had done to Egypt and to the kings east of the Jordan (9:9-10). Convinced that defeat was certain, they sought survival through deception.

The deception of the Gibeonites (9:3-15)

The Gibeonites devised a clever ruse. They sent a delegation to Joshua at Gilgal "with worn-out sacks for their donkeys, and wineskins, worn-out and torn and mended, with worn-out, patched sandals on their feet, and worn-out clothes, and all their provisions were dry and crumbly" (9:4-5). Every detail was designed to make them appear as travelers from a distant land. When they arrived, they said to Joshua, "We have come from a distant country, so now make a covenant with us" (9:6).

Israel was cautious at first. "Perhaps you live among us; then how can we make a covenant with you?" (9:7). God's law forbade treaties with the nations of Canaan (Deut. 7:1-2), for such alliances would lead to compromise and idolatry. Yet the Gibeonites persisted, claiming, "We are your servants … from a very distant country your servants have come because of the name of the Lord your God" (9:8–9). They flattered Israel by acknowledging the Lord's fame, though their motives were self-preserving rather than faithful.

To prove their story, they presented their supplies: "Here is our bread; it was still warm when we took it from our houses … but now, behold, it is dry and crumbly" (9:12). The deception was thorough. Yet the narrative turns on a tragic phrase: "So the men took some of their provisions, but did not ask counsel from the Lord" (9:14).

This was the heart of Israel's failure. Joshua and the leaders relied on their senses rather than on divine guidance. The evidence seemed convincing, but discernment without prayer is dangerous. Even wise and faithful people err when they neglect to seek God's direction. Joshua made peace with the Gibeonites and confirmed the treaty with an oath before the Lord (9:15). The covenant, though made in ignorance, was binding because it had been sworn in God's name.

The deception revealed (9:16–21)

Three days later, the truth came to light. "They heard that they were their neighbors and that they lived among them" (9:16). Israel set out and came to the cities of Gibeon, Chephirah, Beeroth, and Kiriath-jearim, but did not attack them. "Because the leaders of the congregation had sworn to them by the Lord, the God of Israel, then all the congregation murmured against the leaders" (9:18).

The people were angry that their leaders had been deceived, but Joshua and the elders refused to break the oath. "We have sworn to them by the Lord, the God of Israel, and now we may not touch them" (9:19). To violate the covenant would be to dishonor God's name. The leaders instead pronounced a sentence of servitude: "Let them live, but let them be cutters of wood and drawers of water for all the congregation" (9:21).

This decision upheld both justice and mercy. Though the treaty had been made under false pretenses, it had been sworn before God, whose name must never be treated lightly. Centuries later, King Saul's violation of this oath brought judgment on Israel (2 Sam. 21:1–2). God takes vows seriously—even those made in error—because they reflect his unchanging truthfulness.

Joshua confronts the Gibeonites (9:22-27)

Joshua summoned the deceivers and demanded an explanation. "Why did you deceive us, saying, 'We are very far from you,' when you dwell among us?" (9:22). The Gibeonites answered honestly: "It was told to your servants for a certainty that the Lord your God had commanded his servant Moses to give you all the land … so we feared greatly for our lives" (9:24). Their deceit arose from fear, not defiance. They believed the Lord's promises enough to act on them—though imperfectly.

Joshua spared their lives but assigned them to permanent servitude: "You are cursed, and some of you shall never be anything but servants, cutters of wood and drawers of water for the house of my God" (9:23). This punishment fit both the offense and the mercy granted. They would live, but their labor would constantly remind them of their deception. Remarkably, their role placed them near the tabernacle, where they would daily witness Israel's worship of the true God. Later in Scripture, the Gibeonites (also called the Nethinim) appear as faithful temple servants after the exile (Ezra 2:43-58). God's mercy turned their curse into a calling.

The story ends on a note of balance: justice without vengeance, mercy without compromise. Israel kept its word, and God preserved his honor. The Gibeonites lived as humble servants, and Israel learned the cost of neglecting divine guidance.

Theological reflections

Joshua 9 provides a sobering study in discernment, integrity, and the mercy of God. First, *spiritual discernment requires prayer.* The tragedy of this chapter rests on verse 14: "They did not ask counsel from the Lord." The deception succeeded because Israel relied on evidence rather than revelation. Even experienced leaders fail when they trust their judgment instead of seeking God's direction. Wisdom begins with prayerful dependence.

Second, *truthfulness before God matters more than convenience.* Joshua honored the treaty because it had been sworn by the Lord's name. Breaking it would have profaned the covenant. In a world that treats promises lightly, God calls his people to be faithful to their word, even when keeping it is costly. Integrity reflects the character of the God we serve.

Third, *God's mercy extends even to those outside the covenant.* The Gibeonites, though deceitful, expressed faith in the Lord's power. Their survival illustrates God's willingness to show grace to those who seek refuge in him. Like Rahab, they turned from certain destruction to humble service among God's people.

Finally, *God can redeem even our mistakes.* Israel's failure became a lesson in grace. Though deceived, they honored their word, and the Gibeonites were brought near to God's worship. The Lord often transforms our blunders into blessings when we repent and remain faithful. What begins in failure can end in faithfulness if we submit to his mercy.

APPLICATION

1. Seek God's counsel before making decisions

Israel's mistake was not their compassion but their carelessness. "They did not ask counsel from the Lord." Everything about the Gibeonites' story looked convincing—the worn clothes, the moldy bread, the humble speech. But appearances can deceive, and good intentions cannot replace prayer. Joshua and the leaders acted on observation instead of revelation. The same danger faces Christians today. We often make choices based on what seems reasonable, forgetting to seek God's guidance through prayer and Scripture. Wisdom requires dependence, not confidence in our own judgment. God's will is not discovered through haste but through humility. When we pause to seek his direction, we invite his protection. Every decision, whether large or small, should begin with the question, "Lord, what do you will?" A moment of prayer can prevent a lifetime of regret.

2. Honor your word even when it costs you

Joshua's leaders quickly realized they had been deceived, yet they refused to break their oath. "We have sworn to them by the Lord, and now we may not touch them." Integrity demanded that they keep their promise, even though it had been made in error. Their example teaches that God's people must be people of their word. In a world where commitments are easily broken, faithfulness to promises displays the character of Christ. Marriage vows, business agreements, and church responsibilities all fall under the same principle. When we give our word, we represent the God of truth. Joshua's obedience brought peace to his conscience and honor to God's name. Keeping our word may bring inconvenience or cost, but it brings something far greater—credibility before the world and approval before the Lord.

3. God's mercy reaches even the undeserving

The Gibeonites gained mercy through deceit, yet God allowed them to live and even serve near his sanctuary. Their survival was not a reward for dishonesty but a demonstration of grace. God often shows mercy to those who least deserve it—people like us. The Gibeonites feared judgment and sought refuge, however imperfectly, in the God of Israel. Their story reminds us that divine compassion outweighs human failure. The cross of Christ fulfills this truth completely: sinners who approach in humility and faith find life instead of death. Christians must reflect that same grace toward others, remembering that we too are former outsiders brought near by mercy. God can redeem even those who come with mixed motives if they come seeking his mercy. His grace turns deception into devotion and foreigners into servants in his house.

4. God can redeem our mistakes for his glory

Joshua's decision to make a treaty with Gibeon was a failure in discernment, but God turned it into an opportunity for grace. The Gibeonites later served faithfully in Israel's worship (Neh. 3:7). What began as error ended in blessing because Joshua honored his oath and God remained merciful. Christians today can take hope from this. Our missteps do not end God's plans; his sovereignty can weave even our failures into his purposes. Repentance and integrity invite redemption. When we acknowledge our error and keep trusting the Lord, he transforms shame into service and folly into faithfulness. The key is humility—owning our mistakes, learning from them, and letting God write a better ending than we deserve. His grace not only forgives failure; it restores purpose beyond it.

CONCLUSION

The story of the Gibeonites reminds us that wisdom without prayer soon becomes presumption. Joshua's failure was not in kindness but in carelessness—he trusted his eyes instead of the Lord. Yet even amid error, God's grace prevailed. Israel kept its covenant, God's name was honored, and the

Gibeonites were drawn near to serve at his sanctuary. The Lord turned a blunder into a blessing. For Christians, this chapter offers both warning and comfort: we must seek God's will before acting, but when we fail, repentance and integrity can still bring redemption. The God who guided Joshua after deception continues to guide his people through mercy. When we seek his counsel and walk in his truth, he transforms even our misjudgments into testimony. His faithfulness endures when ours falters.

REFLECTION

1. Why did Israel fail to recognize the Gibeonites' deception?
2. What does it mean to "ask counsel from the Lord" in daily decisions?
3. How can believers practice honesty even when it costs them?
4. What does this story teach about God's faithfulness when we make mistakes?
5. When have you seen God redeem an error for his glory?
6. How can the Gibeonites' mercy encourage you about grace today?

DISCUSSION

1. What lessons about discernment does Joshua 9 offer to church leaders today?
2. Why is integrity before God more important than convenience or reputation?
3. How can prayer protect us from being deceived by appearances?
4. What does Joshua's treatment of the Gibeonites reveal about honoring God's name?
5. In what ways does this story foreshadow the inclusion of Gentiles in God's plan?
6. How can the church turn past mistakes into opportunities for service and redemption?

9

THE LONG DAY OF BATTLE

JOSHUA 10

Objective: To prove that God fights for his people, answering faith-filled prayers and turning weakness into victory.

INTRODUCTION

In June 1940, as the Allied armies retreated toward the French coast, British Prime Minister Winston Churchill faced the darkest moment of World War II. Surrounded by the enemy, with thousands of soldiers trapped on the beaches of Dunkirk, he ordered an unlikely rescue. Civilian ships—fishing boats, ferries, and yachts—crossed the English Channel and saved more than 300,000 men. Later, Churchill called it "a miracle of deliverance." When human strength failed, courage and providence met in the same moment.

Joshua 10 describes a miracle of deliverance on an even grander scale. Five Amorite kings united to destroy Gibeon, and Joshua marched all night to defend them. God intervened with hailstones from heaven and even made the sun stand still so Israel could finish the victory. What began as a flawed alliance became the stage for one of the greatest displays of divine power in Scripture.

This "long day" teaches that God is never bound by time, circumstance, or human weakness. When his people trust him, he fights for them in ways they could never imagine. Joshua's prayer and God's answer remind believers that the Creator still commands creation and that victory always belongs to the Lord who hears and helps his people.

EXAMINATION

The alliance of kings (10:1-5)

The Gibeonite treaty of chapter 9 sent shockwaves through Canaan. When Adoni-zedek, king of Jerusalem, learned that Gibeon had made peace with Israel, he realized the balance of power had shifted. "Gibeon was a great city, like one of the royal cities ... and all its men were warriors" (10:2). Gibeon's defection not only deprived the southern coalition of a strong ally but also provided Israel a foothold near the heart of the land.

In response, Adoni-zedek formed a military alliance with four other kings: Hoham of Hebron, Piram of Jarmuth, Japhia of Lachish, and Debir of Eglon (10:3). Together they planned to punish Gibeon for its surrender and discourage other cities from seeking peace. "Come up to me and help me, and let us strike Gibeon," Adoni-zedek urged, "for it has made peace with Joshua and with the people of Israel" (10:4). Their goal was to destroy Gibeon and resist God's advancing purposes.

This coalition reveals the hardness of the human heart. Instead of turning to the Lord in repentance after hearing of his power, these kings chose rebellion. Like Pharaoh before them, they gathered their armies to fight against the God of heaven—and sealed their own destruction.

The cry for help (10:6-8)

When the five kings attacked, Gibeon sent an urgent plea to Israel: "Do not relax your hand from your servants. Come up to us quickly and save us and help us" (10:6). Though their treaty had been born from deception, Joshua and Israel were bound by their oath. A covenant sworn in God's name could not be broken. Instead of abandoning the Gibeonites, Joshua responded immediately.

"So Joshua went up from Gilgal, he and all the people of war with him, and all the mighty men of valor" (10:7). God then assured him: "Do not fear them, for I have given them into your hands. Not a man of them shall stand before you" (10:8). The same words of encouragement once spoken before Jericho now resounded again. Joshua had made a mistake with Gibeon, but God still honored integrity and faithfulness. His promise did not depend on perfection but on obedience.

Joshua's compassion and quick response reveal a heart transformed by grace. Instead of holding past deceit against Gibeon, he acted as a faithful protector. God likewise calls his people to show mercy to those who seek refuge, even when their past is imperfect.

The surprise attack (10:9–11)

Joshua marched his army all night from Gilgal—a journey of about twenty miles uphill—and took the enemy by surprise. "And the Lord threw them into a panic before Israel, who struck them with a great blow at Gibeon" (10:10). The enemy's confusion was no accident; it was divine intervention. God himself fought for Israel.

As the Canaanites fled down the road from Beth-horon toward Azekah and Makkedah, "the Lord threw down large stones from heaven on them … and there were more who died because of the hailstones than the sons of Israel killed with the sword" (10:11). The hailstorm was both miraculous and symbolic—a reminder that victory belongs to God alone. Just as he had drowned Egypt's army in the Red Sea, now he hurled hail from heaven to defend his people. Nature itself became a weapon in the hands of its Creator.

The scene emphasizes divine sovereignty in human conflict. Israel fought valiantly, but the decisive blows came from God. He not only strengthens his people's efforts but multiplies them with his own power. When Christians fight the battles of faith, their strength is never enough; yet with God, victory is certain.

The long day (10:12–15)

As the battle continued, Joshua prayed one of the most remarkable prayers in Scripture: "Sun, stand still at Gibeon, and moon, in the Valley of Aijalon" (10:12). The text records, "And the sun stood still, and the moon stopped, until the nation took vengeance on their enemies" (10:13). The writer adds, "There has been no day like it before or since, when the Lord heeded the voice of a man, for the Lord fought for Israel" (10:14).

The language portrays a unique extension of daylight that allowed Israel to complete its victory. Whether God literally halted the earth's rotation, refracted sunlight, or prolonged the battle through supernatural light, the meaning is clear: God controls time and creation for the sake of his people. Joshua's faith was bold, yet his prayer was rooted in purpose—he asked for more daylight to finish the task God had given. God's power responded to a prayer aligned with his mission.

This episode reminds us that prayer can move heaven when it serves God's will. Joshua's confidence flowed from his knowledge of God's promise. The God who commands the universe is not distant; he listens to the cries of his servants. The Lord who made the sun stand still for Joshua still works wonders for those who trust and obey him.

The defeat of the five kings (10:16–27)

The five kings fled and hid themselves in a cave at Makkedah. When Joshua learned of it, he ordered large stones rolled across the cave's mouth to trap them while the army pursued their fleeing forces (10:17–19). After the battle was complete, Joshua returned and had the kings brought before him. He summoned his commanders and said, "Come near; put your feet on the necks of these kings" (10:24). The gesture symbolized total victory and the fulfillment of God's promise: "The Lord will do to all your enemies against whom you fight" (10:25).

Joshua then executed the kings and hanged their bodies on trees until evening, afterward placing them in the cave and sealing it with stones (10:26–27). The scene may seem grim, but it demonstrates that the conquest was an act of divine judgment, not human vengeance. The kings represented the collective rebellion of Canaan against the Lord. Their defeat assured Israel that God's word was certain and his justice complete.

The southern campaign (10:28–43)

Following the victory at Makkedah, Joshua launched a rapid campaign through southern Canaan. In succession, Israel captured and destroyed Makkedah, Libnah, Lachish, Eglon, Hebron, and Debir. Each battle followed the same pattern: "Joshua captured it ... and he left none remaining, but devoted it to destruction, just as the Lord God of Israel commanded" (10:28–39). The repetition underscores total obedience. Unlike the earlier defeat at Ai, Israel now acted in full alignment with God's word.

These victories were not merely territorial; they fulfilled God's covenant promise to Abraham—to give his descendants the land. The campaign concluded with a summary statement: "So Joshua struck the whole land ... and left none remaining, but devoted to destruction all that breathed, just as the Lord God of Israel commanded. And Joshua returned, and all Israel with him, to the camp at Gilgal" (10:40–43).

This passage highlights the completeness of God's faithfulness. Every promise given to Joshua at the outset—"No man shall be able to stand before you" (1:5)—was now realized. Yet these victories also carry moral weight. The destruction of the Canaanites was an expression of divine justice, not ethnic prejudice. Their sins—idolatry, violence, and immorality—had long provoked the Lord's patience (Gen. 15:16). The conquest was both judgment on sin and mercy for future generations, establishing a land where holiness and worship could flourish.

Theological reflections

Joshua 10 reveals the power of a faithful God who fights for his people and fulfills every promise. First, **God is sovereign over creation**. The sun, moon, and hail all obey his command. The universe itself serves his redemptive purposes. Believers can take comfort that nothing in creation—time, weather, or circumstance—lies beyond his control.

Second, **God honors integrity even after failure**. Joshua had made peace with Gibeon unwisely, yet his faithfulness to that covenant led to a greater victory. The Lord rewards those who keep their word, even when it is costly.

Third, **God responds to the prayers of faith**. Joshua's bold petition for the sun to stand still demonstrates that prayer aligned with God's will can accomplish the impossible. God invites his people to pray big prayers that advance his purposes.

Fourth, **God fights for those who trust him**. The hailstones, the panic, and the extended day all testify that the battle belongs to the Lord. Israel's effort mattered, but God's power decided the outcome.

Finally, **God's judgment is real, but his mercy is greater**. The same Lord who judged Canaan's kings offers salvation through Christ to all nations. The long day at Gibeon foreshadows the greater victory of the cross, where the Son of God conquered sin once and for all. The God who commands the sun to stand still still shines light into the darkness of human hearts.

APPLICATION

1. God fights for those who are faithful to his word

Joshua honored the covenant with Gibeon even though it had been made through deception. His faithfulness brought divine help, proving that integrity invites God's favor. When Christians keep their word and walk in righteousness, the Lord fights on their behalf. The hailstorm, panic, and extended sunlight were not random acts of nature—they were responses to covenant loyalty. Christians can trust that God still defends those who stand by truth even when others break it. He may not send hail from heaven, but his providence still works for our good. When we remain faithful in our commitments, we place ourselves under the shelter of his power. Obedience is not weakness; it is alignment with divine strength. The Lord's victories always accompany the people who honor his word.

2. Prayer moves the hand of God

Joshua's bold request for the sun to stand still reflects a heart confident in God's power. His prayer was not for personal comfort but for the completion of God's mission. God honored that faith because it aligned with his purpose. The same principle holds today: when our prayers seek the advancement of God's will, they unleash his power. Christians often limit their prayers to what seems reasonable, forgetting that the Lord who governs time and creation still hears. Faith-filled prayer does not manipulate God; it cooperates with him. The prayer of the righteous, James writes, "has great power as it is working" (Jas. 5:16). Joshua's long day reminds us that no prayer is too bold when it serves God's glory. The God who controls the sun still listens to the cries of his people.

3. Victory belongs to the Lord, not to us

The victory at Gibeon came not through superior skill but through divine action. The Lord threw the enemy into panic and rained down hailstones from heaven, killing more than Israel's swords ever could. God's people fought bravely, yet the credit belonged entirely to him. Christians must remember that success in spiritual battles—whether overcoming sin, spreading the gospel, or enduring trials—comes only by God's strength. Pride tempts us to believe our plans or persistence guarantee results, but every triumph is a gift of grace. We march, we fight, we pray, but the Lord brings victory. When we give him the glory, our faith deepens and our hearts remain humble. The long day of Joshua teaches that the greatest victories happen when God's people rely completely on his power.

4. God can turn human mistakes into opportunities for grace

The alliance with Gibeon began in error, yet God used it to demonstrate his faithfulness. Joshua's decision to keep his oath brought about the southern campaign that secured the land. What started as a compromise ended in conquest. God often redeems our missteps when we repent and continue walking in obedience. Christians can take comfort that their failures do not cancel God's purposes. The Lord is a master of turning weakness into witness, defeat into dependence, and mistakes into mercy. When we yield our regrets to him, he weaves them into his redemptive story. Joshua's flawed treaty became the doorway to Israel's greatest victory—proof that grace wastes nothing surrendered to God. Our brokenness, once offered to him, becomes a platform for his glory.

CONCLUSION

The long day at Gibeon stands as one of Scripture's greatest testaments to God's power and faithfulness. When Joshua prayed, God heard. When Israel obeyed, God acted. The sun stood still, hail fell from heaven, and the enemies of God's people were destroyed. Yet the greater lesson lies beyond the miracle itself—it is that the Lord still fights for those who walk in faith. The same God who lengthened a day to complete victory continues to move heaven and earth for his children. Joshua's courage, prayer, and obedience reveal the path to triumph: trust God's promise, act in faith, and give him glory. When the battle seems too great and the night too near, the Lord remains mighty to save. His light still shines, and his victories never fade.

REFLECTION

1. What does God's command, "Do not fear," reveal about his heart toward his people?

2. Why was Joshua willing to defend the Gibeonites despite their earlier deception?

3. How does this chapter strengthen your faith in the power of prayer?

4. What does the "long day" teach you about God's control over creation and time?

5. When have you seen God turn a past mistake into an opportunity for grace?

6. How can Joshua's courage inspire your trust in God's promises today?

DISCUSSION

1. What does Joshua's faith in asking for the sun to stand still teach about prayer aligned with God's will?

2. Why did God choose to fight for Israel using hailstones and extended daylight?

3. How does Joshua's treatment of the five kings illustrate divine justice and leadership?

4. What lessons about integrity and mercy continue from the covenant with Gibeon?

5. How does Joshua 10 foreshadow God's ultimate victory through Christ?

6. What practical ways can the church today show confidence that "the Lord fights for us"?

10

REST FROM WAR

JOSHUA 11–12

Objective: To show that obedience and perseverance bring rest through the faithfulness of God's promises.

INTRODUCTION

In 1918, after more than four years of brutal conflict, the guns of World War I finally fell silent. Across Europe, soldiers who had endured unimaginable hardship laid down their weapons as church bells rang in celebration. The armistice did not erase the scars of war, but for the first time in years, the world exhaled. The long struggle was over—peace, however fragile, had come.

Joshua 11–12 records a similar moment of divine relief. After years of relentless battle—from Jericho to Hazor—Israel finally experienced rest. "So Joshua took the whole land … and the land had rest from war." God's promises to Abraham had been fulfilled. The armies of Canaan were defeated, the kings subdued, and the people could now dwell in the land God had sworn to give them. Yet this rest was more than political—it was spiritual.

Israel's rest pointed forward to something greater: the rest believers find in Christ. Just as Joshua led God's people into a land of promise, Jesus leads his followers into the peace of redemption. True rest does not come through conquest but through communion with God. The story of Joshua's final battles reminds us that faith's struggles end not in exhaustion but in fulfillment—the peace that comes when God finishes what he began.

EXAMINATION

The northern coalition (11:1–5)

Following Israel's victories in the south, Jabin, king of Hazor, formed a vast alliance of northern kings to resist Joshua. "Hazor was the head of all those kingdoms" (11:10), a powerful city located north of the Sea of Galilee. Jabin sent word to the kings of Madon, Shimron, Achshaph, and many others across the hill country, the Jordan Valley, and the coasts near Mount Hermon. Their armies were immense—"a great horde, in number like the sand that is on the seashore, with very many horses and chariots" (11:4).

The southern kings had fallen one by one; the northern kings now joined forces to face Israel collectively. Yet their unity could not overcome their rebellion. They gathered at the waters of Merom to fight, unaware that their greatest enemy was not Israel's army but the Lord himself. Human alliances may seem strong, but they cannot stand against God's purposes.

The Lord's assurance and Israel's attack (11:6–9)

Once again, the Lord encouraged Joshua: "Do not be afraid of them, for tomorrow at this time I will give over all of them, slain, to Israel" (11:6). Despite the size and sophistication of the enemy—with horses and chariots far superior to Israel's weapons—God promised victory. He also commanded Joshua to cripple their military power: "You shall hamstring their horses and burn their chariots with fire."

The next day, Joshua launched a surprise attack at the waters of Merom. "And the Lord gave them into the hand of Israel, who struck them and chased them ... until they left none remaining" (11:8). The horses were hamstrung and the chariots burned, ensuring that Israel would not place its trust in military technology. Their dependence was to rest on God alone.

This encounter demonstrates the recurring pattern of Joshua's leadership: divine command, human obedience, and divine victory. God's word guaranteed success, but Israel still had to act in faith. True courage arises not from confidence in one's strength but from conviction in God's promises.

The destruction of Hazor (11:10–15)

After the victory at Merom, Joshua captured Hazor, "the head of all those kingdoms," and struck down its king (11:10). The city was burned, but the other towns were spared as settlements for Israel (11:13). Hazor's destruction was decisive—it symbolized the collapse of organized Canaanite resistance in the north.

The narrator emphasizes Joshua's complete obedience: "Just as the Lord had commanded Moses his servant, so Moses commanded Joshua, and so Joshua did. He left nothing undone of all that the Lord had commanded Moses" (11:15). This statement captures the essence of Joshua's leadership. His greatness did not lie in innovation but in submission. God's servant triumphed because he followed the revealed word without deviation.

The judgment on Hazor and its allies fulfilled God's long-standing promise to Abraham (Gen. 15:16). The time of mercy had passed, and Canaan's iniquity had reached its limit. These conquests, often misunderstood, were not acts of cruelty but of divine justice against idolatry and violence. The Canaanites' destruction safeguarded Israel's holiness and preserved the covenant line through which the Messiah would come.

The long obedience of conquest (11:16–23)

The remainder of Joshua 11 summarizes years of warfare. "So Joshua took all that land, the hill country and all the Negeb and all the land of Goshen and the lowland and the Arabah ... and all their kings he captured and struck them down" (11:16–17). The campaign was not swift; "Joshua made war a long time with all those kings" (11:18). Victory was certain but not immediate. God's promises demanded perseverance.

No peace was made with any of the Canaanite nations except the Gibeonites, "for it was the Lord's doing to harden their hearts that they should come against Israel in battle, in order that they should be devoted to destruction" (11:20). Like Pharaoh in Exodus, the kings' hard hearts revealed both their guilt and God's sovereignty. Judgment came not because God desired destruction but because they persistently rejected mercy.

The chapter closes with a note of rest: "So Joshua took the whole land ... and the land had rest from war" (11:23). The rest was not permanent peace but a divine pause. Israel's enemies were subdued, the conquest complete, and God's promise fulfilled. The phrase anticipates the spiritual rest believers find in Christ (Heb. 4:8–10)—a rest secured not by human effort but by divine victory.

The list of defeated kings (12:1–24)

Joshua 12 catalogs the kings defeated by Israel. The first section (12:1–6) recalls Moses' victories east of the Jordan: Sihon of Heshbon and Og of Bashan. These conquests had prepared the way for Israel's entrance into Canaan. The second section (12:7–24) lists thirty-one kings defeated by Joshua west of the Jordan. From Jericho to Hazor, each fallen king testified to God's faithfulness.

Though these lists may seem repetitive, they serve an important theological purpose. Every name represents a fulfilled promise. What God had sworn to Abraham centuries earlier was now reality. The enumeration of kings transforms history into testimony: "See what the Lord has done." The long list is not tedious—it is triumphant.

The record also contrasts God's enduring faithfulness with human frailty. Kings rise and fall, but the Lord remains sovereign. The nations trusted in walls, weapons, and alliances; Israel trusted in the word of God—and prevailed. Joshua's obedience brought closure to a generation of promise and prepared the way for the division of the land among the tribes.

Theological reflections

Joshua 11–12 marks the conclusion of Israel's conquest and the fulfillment of God's promise to give them the land. Several theological truths emerge from these chapters.

First, *God's promises may be delayed but never denied*. The conquest took years, yet every promise to Abraham, Isaac, and Jacob was fulfilled exactly as spoken. Faith must endure through long seasons of struggle, trusting that God's timing is perfect.

Second, *obedience ensures victory*. The summary of Joshua's work—"he left nothing undone of all that the Lord commanded"—reminds believers that success in God's kingdom flows from faithfulness, not innovation. God blesses the hands of those who obey his word completely.

Third, *divine judgment reveals divine holiness*. The destruction of Canaan was not racial or political but moral and spiritual. God's patience had run its course, and justice required judgment. Yet even in wrath, mercy remained available to those, like Rahab or the Gibeonites, who turned to the Lord in faith.

Fourth, *rest follows obedience*. The phrase "the land had rest from war" echoes the deeper rest God provides to his people—a rest of trust, reconciliation, and peace. This physical rest prefigured the spiritual rest Jesus offers to all who come to him (Matt. 11:28).

Finally, *God's faithfulness deserves remembrance*. The long list of kings in chapter 12 reminds believers that every victory belongs to the Lord. Our memories must hold both the battles and the blessings so that future generations may know that God keeps his word.

APPLICATION

1. God's promises require patience and perseverance

Joshua's campaigns in Canaan were not accomplished overnight. "Joshua made war a long time with all those kings." Victory took years, not days. Yet every promise God made was fulfilled exactly as he said. Faith does not exempt believers from endurance; it demands it. Many Christians grow weary when progress feels slow, forgetting that spiritual maturity and divine promises unfold over time. God's work in our lives often takes longer than we expect but always ends better than we imagine. The key is to keep obeying while we wait. Perseverance proves trust more than passion does. As Joshua's long obedience led to rest, so patient faith leads believers to the peace Christ provides. God's promises are certain, but his schedule is sovereign. Our task is not to rush his timing but to remain steadfast until the victory comes.

2. Obedience is the measure of success

Joshua's greatness was summed up in one simple line: "He left nothing undone of all that the Lord had commanded Moses." His victories were not the result of strategy, charisma, or luck—they came through complete obedience. God measures success by faithfulness, not numbers or recognition. The same principle governs the church today. Ministries flourish not through clever planning but through humble submission to God's word. When believers obey the commands of Scripture—preaching the gospel, serving others, and walking in holiness—the Lord provides fruit in his time. Obedience is not glamorous, but it is powerful. Each act of faith builds upon the last until the Lord's purposes are accomplished. Joshua's legacy reminds us that the highest achievement in God's kingdom is to finish the work he has assigned with nothing left undone.

3. Rest follows surrender, not strength

The final words of chapter 11—"The land had rest from war"—capture the heart of God's promise. Rest did not come from Israel's superiority but from their surrender to God's will. When the fighting ceased, it was because the Lord had delivered the land into their hands. This rest foreshadows the spiritual peace available in Christ. Many strive for peace through success, comfort, or control, but true rest comes only from trusting in God's completed work. When Christians stop fighting against his commands and yield to his authority, they discover a deeper calm than the world can offer. Israel's rest was temporary, but Christ's rest is eternal. To lay down arms before the Lord is not defeat—it is victory. Peace is not achieved by exhaustion but received by faith.

4. Remember what God has done

The long list of thirty-one defeated kings in chapter 12 might seem tedious, but it serves a vital purpose: it records God's faithfulness in detail. Each name was a reminder that the Lord keeps his word. Remembering God's victories strengthens faith for the battles still ahead. Christians often forget yesterday's deliverance and therefore doubt tomorrow's help. Gratitude guards the heart from fear and pride alike. Just as Israel recited their victories, believers should recount God's goodness—through prayer, worship, and testimony. Journaling, communion, and song are all modern memorials of divine faithfulness. When we remember, we worship; and when we worship, our hearts find courage to trust again. Forgetfulness leads to unbelief, but remembrance renews hope. God's record of faithfulness assures us that the story he began will end in triumph.

CONCLUSION

The conquest of Canaan ended where it began—with the faithfulness of God. Every city captured, every king defeated, and every promise fulfilled testified that the Lord keeps his word. Joshua's generation learned that victory was not gained through speed or strength but through steady obedience. The same truth holds for believers today: God's promises require patient trust, but his faithfulness never fails. The rest Israel enjoyed was temporary; ours in Christ is eternal. Through him, we find peace with God and confidence in his unchanging care. As Joshua "left nothing undone of all that the Lord commanded," may we also finish our course in faithfulness, knowing that when the battles of life are over, the Lord will give his people rest.

REFLECTION

1. How does Joshua's perseverance encourage you to trust God's timing?
2. What does it mean to "leave nothing undone" of what God has commanded?
3. Where do you see God's faithfulness in the long battles of your life?
4. How does Israel's rest from war point to the peace found in Christ?
5. Why is remembering God's past victories essential to spiritual growth?
6. How can you rest more deeply in God's promises this week?

DISCUSSION

1. Why did God require Joshua to fight for years when victory was already promised?
2. How do chapters 11–12 reveal the balance between divine sovereignty and human effort?
3. What can the church learn from Joshua's complete obedience?
4. Why does Scripture often link rest with faith and obedience?
5. How can Christians today "hamstring the horses" that tempt them to trust human strength?
6. What practices help believers remember and celebrate God's faithfulness?

11

THE LAND DIVIDED

JOSHUA 13–21

Objective: To prove that God's faithfulness provides every promise, but faith must claim what grace supplies.

INTRODUCTION

In 1862, during the height of the American frontier expansion, President Abraham Lincoln signed the Homestead Act, granting 160 acres of public land to settlers willing to cultivate it. Thousands claimed the promise, but many failed to make it their own. Harsh weather, isolation, and discouragement caused some to abandon what was freely offered. The land was theirs in law—but only those who labored in faith possessed it in reality.

Israel faced a similar challenge in the days of Joshua. After years of conquest, God had given them the land he promised to Abraham. The battles were largely over, but much remained to be claimed. The time had come to move from war to inheritance, from fighting to faithfulness. Joshua's task was not only to lead soldiers but to help tribes take hold of what God had already given.

The dividing of the land reminds believers that God's promises must be personally possessed. He provides salvation, peace, and blessing—but faith must step forward to claim them. Just as Joshua's generation learned to live in the land of promise, Christians today must learn to live in the promises of God. The story of Joshua 13–21 calls us from hesitation to inheritance, from wandering to rest.

EXAMINATION

Unfinished business and God's command (13:1–7)

After years of conquest, Israel stood on the brink of fulfillment. "Now Joshua was old and advanced in years, and the Lord said to him, 'You are old and advanced in years, and there remains yet very much land to possess'" (13:1). Though the major battles had been won, scattered strongholds still remained. God's promise was sure, but its full enjoyment required continued faithfulness. Joshua's task shifted from warrior to administrator—to distribute the land as inheritance for the tribes.

The Lord's words reaffirmed both his sovereignty and his generosity. "I myself will drive them out from before the people of Israel. Only allot the land to Israel for an inheritance, as I have commanded you" (13:6). Joshua's role was to divide what God had already given. The inheritance was guaranteed, but the people would have to claim it by faith and perseverance. The book of Joshua's second half moves from conquest to settlement, from battlefields to boundaries. The same God who grants victory also grants possession.

The inheritance east of the Jordan (13:8–33)

The chapter first records the territory given to the tribes of Reuben, Gad, and the half-tribe of Manasseh east of the Jordan. Moses had already assigned these lands after the defeat of Sihon and Og (Num. 32; Deut. 3). These tribes chose to settle where their livestock could thrive, but their choice also placed them farther from the tabernacle and the center of worship. Though their inheritance was legitimate, it carried risk—the danger of drifting spiritually from their brethren.

The text carefully notes that the Levites received no portion of land: "The Lord God of Israel is their inheritance, just as he said to them" (13:33). This statement becomes a central theological theme throughout the division narratives. The Levites' lack of territory was not deprivation but devotion. Their inheritance was service to the Lord. Their dependence on

God's provision through the other tribes illustrated that spiritual privilege outweighs material possession.

The inheritance of Caleb (14:6-15)

Chapter 14 highlights Caleb, a model of enduring faith. Decades earlier, he and Joshua had stood alone among the twelve spies, believing that God could give Israel the land (Num. 13-14). Now, at eighty-five years old, Caleb approached Joshua and said, "I am still as strong today as I was in the day that Moses sent me ... So now give me this hill country of which the Lord spoke on that day" (14:11-12). His request focused on Hebron, a region still inhabited by the Anakim—the giants who once terrified Israel.

Caleb's courage rested on God's promise, not personal strength: "It may be that the Lord will be with me, and I shall drive them out just as the Lord said" (14:12). Joshua blessed him, and Hebron became his inheritance. The text concludes, "Therefore Hebron became the inheritance of Caleb ... because he wholly followed the Lord, the God of Israel" (14:14). Caleb's story contrasts sharply with the fear of earlier generations. Faithful perseverance claims the promises that unbelief forfeits.

The allotment by lot (15:1-19:51)

The following chapters detail the distribution of land among the remaining tribes, beginning with Judah (15), then Joseph's sons—Ephraim and Manasseh (16-17)—and finally the remaining seven tribes (18-19). Although these boundaries may seem repetitive, they reveal both order and fairness. The land was allotted by lot before the Lord at Shiloh (18:6, 10). The process ensured that divine providence, not human preference, determined each tribe's inheritance.

Judah's allotment in the south included Hebron and the cities later associated with David's reign. The tribes of Ephraim and Manasseh received rich agricultural regions in central Canaan but struggled to fully expel the Canaanites (16:10; 17:12-13). When the remaining tribes delayed taking possession, Joshua rebuked them: "How long will you put off going in to take possession of the land that the Lord, the God of your fathers, has given you?" (18:3). Complacency threatened to undo the progress faith had achieved.

The completion of the allotment signified both fulfillment and responsibility. God had been faithful to his word, but his people were called to live faithfully within that gift. Possession brought privilege—and accountability.

The inheritance of Joshua (19:49–51)

After everyone else had received their inheritance, "the people of Israel gave an inheritance among them to Joshua the son of Nun" (19:49). In humility, Joshua waited until all others were settled before accepting his portion. He chose the city of Timnath-serah in the hill country of Ephraim, where he built and lived (19:50). Like Caleb, Joshua's faithfulness was rewarded with rest in the land he had helped conquer.

The order of events underscores Joshua's servant leadership. He did not claim privilege or priority but received his inheritance as one among his brethren. His example anticipates Christ, who "did not come to be served but to serve" (Matt. 20:28). Leadership in God's kingdom is marked by patience, humility, and obedience. Joshua's faithfulness at the end of his life mirrored his faithfulness at the beginning.

The cities of refuge (20:1–9)

God then commanded the establishment of six cities of refuge—three on each side of the Jordan—where anyone who killed a person unintentionally could flee for safety. "The manslayer who strikes any person without intent … may flee there, and they shall be for you a refuge from the avenger of blood" (20:3). These cities embodied both justice and mercy: justice, because intentional murder was still punished; mercy, because the innocent were protected from vengeance until due process occurred.

The system of refuge illustrated God's concern for human life and fairness. It also foreshadowed the gospel. Just as the fugitive found safety within the city's walls, sinners find refuge in Christ, who protects us from the judgment we deserve. The cities were accessible to all, emphasizing that God's mercy is open to everyone who seeks it.

The cities of the Levites (21:1–45)

The final section details how forty-eight cities were distributed among the Levites, scattered throughout the land. This arrangement ensured that spiritual instruction and worship remained central in every region. The priests and Levites were not isolated; they were interwoven among the tribes as constant reminders of God's presence and law.

The chapter ends with one of the most significant summaries in the entire book: "Thus the Lord gave to Israel all the land that he swore to give to their fathers. And they took possession of it, and they settled there. And the Lord gave them rest on every side … Not one word of all the good promises that the Lord had made to the house of Israel had failed; all came to pass" (21:43–45).

This declaration serves as the theological climax of Joshua. Every battle, boundary, and blessing leads to this truth: God keeps his word. The book that began with "Be strong and courageous" ends with complete fulfillment. Israel's story from promise to possession confirms that divine faithfulness never fails.

Theological reflections

Joshua 13–21 transforms geography into theology, reminding believers that God's promises are both personal and practical.

First, *God fulfills every promise in his time.* Decades after leaving Egypt, Israel now possessed the land. What God begins, he finishes. His promises may unfold slowly, but they never fail.

Second, *faith must claim what grace provides.* The land was a gift, yet Israel had to take possession. Grace offers; faith receives. Christians likewise must live intentionally in the blessings of God's covenant, not merely acknowledge them.

Third, *spiritual inheritance is greater than material gain.* The Levites' portion was the Lord himself—a reminder that the ultimate blessing is communion with God. Our true inheritance is not property or prosperity but fellowship with Christ.

Fourth, *obedience brings rest.* Caleb's courage, Joshua's humility, and Israel's faithfulness led to peace in the land. The rest God gives is not idleness but fulfillment—the settled joy of living in his will.

Finally, *God's faithfulness demands remembrance.* The closing declaration of Joshua 21:45 stands as a monument of divine reliability. In every generation, believers can echo the same testimony: "Not one word of all his promises has failed."

APPLICATION

1. God finishes what he begins

Joshua's final campaigns prove that no promise of God ever fails. "Not one word of all the good promises that the Lord had made … failed; all came to pass." God's faithfulness was not partial but perfect. The same Lord who began Israel's deliverance in Egypt completed it in Canaan. Christians can rest in that same assurance: the God who begins a good work in us will bring it to completion (Phil. 1:6). Our faith often falters in the waiting, but God's timeline is never late. Every unfinished promise of Scripture will one day stand fulfilled. Even when we cannot see progress, we can trust the pattern of divine faithfulness. God does not abandon what he starts. His people may grow weary, but his word endures. The land divided reminds us that God always finishes what grace begins.

2. Faith must claim what grace provides

The Lord had already given the land, yet Joshua challenged the tribes, "How long will you put off going in to take possession of the land that the Lord … has given you?" (18:3). Their hesitation reflects a problem still common among believers—receiving God's promises in word but not in action. Grace offers, but faith must step forward to claim. God's blessings are not theoretical; they are meant to be lived. We can believe in forgiveness yet fail to walk in freedom, or confess trust yet live in fear. Like Israel, many linger at the edge of inheritance. The call of faith is to move in and live fully in what God has provided. Every step of obedience turns promise into experience. What God gives must be possessed through courage, prayer, and persistent faith.

3. True inheritance is found in God himself

When the land was divided, the Levites received no territory because, as Scripture says, "The Lord God of Israel is their inheritance." Their calling reminds believers that the greatest gift is not land, wealth, or comfort—it is fellowship with God. Possessions fade, but communion with the Lord endures. The Levites' dependence on others for provision symbolized that spiritual life depends entirely on God's grace. Christians today share that same inheritance: "'The Lord is my portion,' says my soul, 'therefore I will hope in him'" (Lam. 3:24). The presence of God satisfies what property never can. The tribes enjoyed vineyards and cities; the Levites enjoyed nearness to the altar. The lesson is clear: the richest inheritance belongs to those who serve closest to God. Spiritual intimacy is the believer's true reward.

4. Obedience brings rest and peace

The book's closing declaration—"The Lord gave them rest on every side"—links peace to obedience. Israel's rest came after years of faithfulness and endurance. They followed God's commands, and he fulfilled his word. Peace does not come through avoidance of struggle but through alignment with God's will. When believers walk in obedience, the soul finds stability even amid turmoil. This rest anticipates the greater peace found in Christ, who invites, "Come to me ... and I will give you rest" (Matt. 11:28). Obedience leads to this same rest—a settled assurance that God is in control and that his promises stand secure. Israel's journey from wandering to rest mirrors the Christian pilgrimage from sin to salvation. The battles end when the heart yields completely to God's authority and trusts his unfailing care.

CONCLUSION

The dividing of the land brought Israel to the fulfillment of God's covenant promise. Every boundary, city, and tribe testified that the Lord keeps his word. Yet the story also revealed that possessing the promise required perseverance. Some tribes hesitated, while others—like Caleb and Joshua—stepped forward in faith. God's grace had given them the inheritance; obedience would determine their enjoyment of it.

For Christians, the same truth endures. In Christ, God has already provided every spiritual blessing (Eph. 1:3), but those blessings must be embraced by faith and lived out in obedience. The God who finished his promise to Abraham will finish his work in us. Like Israel, we stand surrounded by grace waiting to be claimed. When faith acts and obedience endures, we find rest, fulfillment, and joy in the God who always keeps his promises.

REFLECTION

1. What does God's faithfulness in Joshua 21:45 teach you about his promises today?
2. How do you see yourself in Israel's hesitation to take full possession of the land?
3. What does Caleb's courage at eighty-five reveal about lifelong faith?
4. How can you claim God's spiritual blessings that you have not yet embraced?
5. Why is fellowship with God a greater inheritance than earthly security?
6. What helps you remember and celebrate God's fulfilled promises in your life?

DISCUSSION

1. Why was it important that the land be divided "by lot before the Lord"?
2. How does the Levites' inheritance illustrate the believer's true portion in Christ?
3. What lessons does Joshua's humility in taking his inheritance last teach about leadership?
4. Why do God's promises sometimes take time and effort to experience fully?
5. In what ways does Israel's rest in Joshua 21 point to the rest Jesus offers today?
6. How can the church encourage one another to live more fully in God's provided blessings?

12

THE ALTAR OF WITNESS
JOSHUA 22

Objective: To affirm that humility, truth, and love preserve unity among God's people and honor his name.

INTRODUCTION

In 1914, as World War I raged across Europe, British and German soldiers faced each other in muddy trenches along the Western Front. Then, on Christmas Eve, something unexpected happened. Soldiers from both sides began singing the same carols—"Silent Night," "O Come, All Ye Faithful." Slowly they emerged from their trenches, shook hands, exchanged gifts, and played soccer in the no-man's-land between them. For one brief moment, the power of shared faith overcame the walls of hostility.

Joshua 22 records a similar moment when misunderstanding nearly destroyed Israel's unity. After years of fighting side by side, the tribes east of the Jordan built a great altar. Their brothers in Canaan misread the act as rebellion, and war almost erupted. Yet through humble conversation and godly wisdom, the truth emerged—the altar was not for division but for remembrance, a witness that "the Lord is God."

This chapter reminds believers that unity is fragile but precious. The people of God must guard it with humility, honesty, and love for the truth.

Misunderstanding will arise, but when hearts remain faithful and communication remains open, God turns potential conflict into deeper fellowship. The altar of witness still speaks: peace and purity walk hand in hand when God's people honor him together.

EXAMINATION

A faithful mission completed (22:1-9)

With the land subdued and the tribes settled, Joshua called together the men of Reuben, Gad, and the half-tribe of Manasseh. These eastern tribes had fulfilled their promise made to Moses years earlier—to cross the Jordan and fight beside their brothers until the land was conquered (Num. 32:16-27). Joshua commended them: "You have kept all that Moses the servant of the Lord commanded you and have obeyed my voice in all that I have commanded you. You have not forsaken your brothers these many days, down to this day, but have been careful to keep the charge of the Lord your God" (22:2-3).

Now that Israel had rest, Joshua released them to return home. Before they departed, he charged them to remain faithful: "Only be very careful to observe the commandment and the law that Moses the servant of the Lord commanded you, to love the Lord your God, and to walk in all his ways and to keep his commandments and to cling to him and to serve him with all your heart and with all your soul" (22:5).

Joshua's words echo the great covenant themes of Deuteronomy—love, obedience, and wholehearted devotion. Obedience was not a condition for grace but the expression of gratitude for it. Joshua blessed them and sent them away with the spoils of war: "Return to your tents with much wealth and with very much livestock, with silver, gold, bronze, and iron, and with much clothing" (22:8). The faithfulness of the eastern tribes modeled unity in purpose and cooperation in God's mission.

A misunderstood altar (22:10-20)

As the eastern tribes returned to their homes across the Jordan, they built a large altar by the river. "When they came to the region of the Jordan that is in the land of Canaan, the people of Reuben and the people of Gad and the half-tribe of Manasseh built there an altar by the Jordan, an altar of imposing size" (22:10). News of this reached the rest of Israel, and alarm spread quickly. The altar seemed to violate God's command that sacrifices be offered only at the tabernacle in Shiloh (Deut. 12:5–14).

The western tribes feared that this act signaled rebellion and idolatry. They gathered at Shiloh to prepare for war against their brothers (22:12). Before attacking, however, they sent a delegation led by Phinehas, the son of Eleazar the priest, along with ten tribal leaders. Their words were direct but reverent: "What is this breach of faith that you have committed against the God of Israel in turning away this day from following the Lord by building yourselves an altar this day in rebellion against the Lord?" (22:16).

The delegation reminded them of Israel's past failures—"the iniquity of Peor" (Num. 25:1–9) and Achan's sin (Josh. 7)—as examples of how one tribe's rebellion could endanger the whole nation (22:17–20). Their response was strong but motivated by concern for holiness. They were determined to preserve Israel's unity around the worship of the one true God.

A faithful explanation (22:21–29)

The eastern tribes responded humbly and truthfully. "The Mighty One, God, the Lord! The Mighty One, God, the Lord! He knows; and let Israel itself know" (22:22). They called on God as their witness that the altar was not for rebellion or sacrifice but for remembrance. They explained, "We did it from fear that in time to come your children might say to our children, 'What have you to do with the Lord, the God of Israel? For the Lord has made the Jordan a boundary between us and you.'" (22:24–25).

The altar was meant as "a witness between us and you, and between our generations after us, that we do perform the service of the Lord in his presence" (22:27). It was not a rival to the altar at Shiloh but a visible testimony of shared faith. The concern of the eastern tribes was legitimate: physical distance could lead to spiritual division. Their solution—a monument of unity—had been misunderstood as rebellion.

Their defense demonstrated humility and clarity. Instead of responding with anger or defensiveness, they appealed to God's knowledge and Israel's conscience. "Far be it from us that we should rebel against the Lord and turn away this day from following the Lord" (22:29). The wisdom of both sides in this exchange prevented civil war. The zeal for purity on one side and the commitment to truth on the other produced peace.

Peace and unity restored (22:30–34)

When Phinehas and the leaders heard the explanation, "it was good in their eyes" (22:30). The misunderstanding was resolved, and reconciliation followed. Phinehas declared, "Today we know that the Lord is in our midst, because you have not committed this breach of faith against the Lord; now you have delivered the people of Israel from the hand of the Lord" (22:31).

The delegation returned to the western tribes and reported the outcome. The people rejoiced and praised God, and war was averted. The chapter concludes: "The people of Reuben and the people of Gad called the altar Witness, for they said, 'It is a witness between us that the Lord is God'" (22:34).

This moment stands as one of the most beautiful resolutions in the Old Testament. What began as a potential civil war ended in worship and unity. Both zeal for truth and grace in communication preserved the fellowship of God's people. Israel learned that misunderstanding, if handled with humility and faith, can become an opportunity for deeper unity.

Theological reflections

Joshua 22 illustrates how easily misunderstanding can fracture God's people—and how faith, communication, and humility can restore peace.

First, *true unity rests on shared devotion to God.* The eastern tribes' altar was not a symbol of division but of belonging. Unity in the Lord is never uniformity of location or culture but loyalty to the same covenant.

Second, *zeal for purity must be guided by love.* The western tribes were right to be concerned about sin, but they first sought dialogue rather than destruction. Their example reminds believers to confront sin firmly but with humility and care.

Third, *communication prevents division.* Israel's leaders pursued understanding before acting, and the result was reconciliation. Many church conflicts today arise not from heresy but from assumption and silence. Honest conversation rooted in love can heal what misunderstanding threatens to destroy.

Fourth, *faithful witness preserves future generations.* The eastern tribes built the altar to remind their descendants of their shared faith. Believers today must also leave memorials—stories, teachings, and examples—that remind the next generation that "the Lord is God."

Finally, *God delights in peace among his people.* The closing joy of Joshua 22 anticipates the unity of the church, where peace through truth glorifies the Lord. The same God who calmed Israel's fear still blesses his people when love and truth dwell together.

APPLICATION

1. True unity is built on shared faithfulness to God

The tribes on both sides of the Jordan were separated by geography but united by covenant. Their unity did not depend on proximity but on loyalty to the same Lord. The altar they built was not a monument to independence but a reminder of belonging. For Christians, the same principle holds true: unity is not uniformity—it is shared devotion to Christ. When believers center their fellowship on the gospel, differences in background, culture, or preference cannot divide them. The church's greatest strength is its common confession that "Jesus is Lord." We must guard that unity through faithfulness to Scripture and love for one another. When devotion to God remains central, distance or difference cannot destroy fellowship. The Lord's people stay one when their hearts are anchored to the same covenant.

2. Zeal for truth must be guided by grace

When the western tribes heard of the altar, they prepared for war but first sought conversation. Their zeal for purity was commendable, yet their restraint was just as crucial. They confronted what seemed to be sin, but they did so through dialogue, not destruction. Christians must learn the same balance. Defending truth is essential, but it must be done in humility and love. Too often believers speak quickly and listen slowly, wounding the very unity they seek to protect. Truth without grace becomes harshness; grace without truth becomes compromise. The gospel calls us to hold both together. The church must be vigilant for sound doctrine, yet gentle in correction, remembering that the goal is restoration, not humiliation. Phinehas' approach reminds us that spiritual maturity seeks peace through honest, compassionate confrontation.

3. Communication prevents unnecessary division

Israel nearly destroyed itself through misunderstanding. The western tribes assumed rebellion; the eastern tribes feared rejection. Only through conversation was the truth revealed. Many modern church conflicts follow the same pattern—assumptions harden into accusations, and relationships fracture before truth is heard. Joshua 22 shows that godly communication can heal what silence destroys. Christians must cultivate patience, humility, and willingness to listen before acting. Talking things through prayerfully often reveals shared faith where division once seemed inevitable. Misunderstandings will arise among God's people, but they need not end in hostility. Honest dialogue guided by Scripture and love protects the unity of Christ's body. The more we speak truthfully and listen graciously, the less ground Satan has to sow discord. Words spoken in faith can build bridges where suspicion once stood.

4. Our witness must endure for future generations

The altar built by the eastern tribes was called "Witness," a lasting reminder that "the Lord is God." Its purpose was to teach future generations about their shared identity as God's people. Every Christian carries that same responsibility. Our faith must not end with us—it must be passed on. The way we worship, teach, and live becomes a witness to those who follow. Parents, teachers, and elders build altars of remembrance through faithful instruction and godly example. When the next generation sees our devotion, they will know that the Lord remains worthy of trust and obedience. The greatest legacy we can leave is not wealth or success but faith that endures. Like the altar at the Jordan, our lives should declare across time and distance: "The Lord is God."

CONCLUSION

Joshua 22 closes the story of conquest with a lesson about community. The altar by the Jordan nearly became the spark of civil war, yet God used humility and honest dialogue to restore peace. Israel learned that unity must be guarded carefully and that misunderstanding can destroy what faith has built. The eastern tribes desired remembrance; the western tribes desired purity. Both were right in motive, and both honored God when they listened. Their reconciliation stands as a model for the church today.

The unity of God's people is not maintained by ignoring differences but by submitting to truth and walking in love. The same Lord who calmed Israel's fear calls his church to preserve "the unity of the Spirit in the bond of peace" (Eph. 4:3). When humility leads our words and God's glory governs our hearts, the altar of witness still stands—a testimony that "the Lord is God."

REFLECTION

1. What does this story teach about how easily misunderstandings can arise among believers?

2. Why was it important for the western tribes to confront the situation before drawing conclusions?

3. How can humility and patience help resolve conflict within the church?

4. What "altars of witness" remind you and others that the Lord is God?

5. How does this chapter show the balance between truth and love in maintaining unity?

6. What steps can you take to preserve unity in your congregation this week?

DISCUSSION

1. Why did the eastern tribes fear that future generations might forget their connection to Israel?

2. How did both sides—east and west—show spiritual maturity in resolving their disagreement?

3. What can church leaders learn from Phinehas' approach to conflict resolution?

4. Why must zeal for doctrinal purity always be tempered by grace and careful listening?

5. How does the altar of witness foreshadow the unity of believers in Christ's church?

6. What practical ways can modern Christians bear witness to their shared faith in God?

13

CHOOSE WHOM YOU WILL SERVE
JOSHUA 23-24

Objective: To call believers to wholehearted devotion by remembering God's faithfulness and choosing to serve him daily.

INTRODUCTION

In 1519, Spanish explorer Hernán Cortés landed on the coast of Mexico with a small army and a daunting mission. Outnumbered and far from home, his men considered turning back. But Cortés famously gave a bold command: "Burn the ships." With no retreat possible, his soldiers had only one option—to move forward. Their commitment changed history.

Joshua issued a similar challenge to Israel at the close of his life. The land was conquered, the people were settled, but a greater battle remained—the battle for their hearts. In his final speech, Joshua reminded them of all God had done and called them to decisive loyalty: "Choose this day whom you will serve." The question was not whether they would serve but whom.

Joshua's words echo through the centuries. Faith is not passive; it demands choice and devotion. Each generation, each believer, must decide where their allegiance lies. The God who had kept every promise now called his people to live in covenant faithfulness. Like Israel, we cannot drift into obedience; we must choose it. Joshua's declaration—"As for me and my house, we will serve the Lord"—still stands as the anthem of every faithful heart.

EXAMINATION

Joshua's farewell and call to faithfulness (23:1-8)

Joshua's final years were marked not by conquest but by counsel. "A long time afterward, when the Lord had given rest to Israel from all their surrounding enemies, and Joshua was old and well advanced in years" (23:1), the faithful leader summoned the nation's elders, heads, judges, and officers. What Moses had done before him, Joshua now did—he delivered a farewell address calling Israel to covenant loyalty.

He began with a reminder of God's faithfulness: "You have seen all that the Lord your God has done to all these nations for your sake, for it is the Lord your God who has fought for you" (23:3). Every victory belonged to the Lord. Joshua's review of the past was not nostalgia but instruction. Memory fuels faithfulness. If Israel remembered what God had done, they would be motivated to continue trusting him.

Joshua then issued a solemn command: "Be very strong to keep and to do all that is written in the Book of the Law of Moses, turning aside from it neither to the right hand nor to the left" (23:6). The same charge God had given Joshua at the beginning of his leadership (1:7-8) now passed to the nation. Success depended not on military power but on moral faithfulness. Israel's rest could only be preserved through obedience.

A warning against compromise (23:9-16)

Joshua praised God's continued presence: "One man of you puts to flight a thousand, since it is the Lord your God who fights for you" (23:10). The Lord's strength was unmatched, but his blessing required devotion: "Be very careful, therefore, to love the Lord your God" (23:11). The warning that followed was stark. If Israel turned back to the gods of the nations or intermarried with them, "know for certain that the Lord your God will no longer drive out these nations before you" (23:13). Compromise would forfeit covenant blessing.

Joshua's words echo the covenant's conditional nature. God's promises of land, peace, and protection were bound to Israel's obedience. Grace had brought them into the land, but faithfulness would determine their continued enjoyment of it. Disobedience would lead to exile and loss—a reality that later generations would tragically experience.

Joshua closed this first address with the same tone of solemnity found in Moses' farewell: "Not one word has failed of all the good things that the Lord your God promised concerning you ... but just as all the good things that the Lord your God promised have been fulfilled, so the Lord will bring upon you all the evil things" (23:14–15). The God who keeps promises of blessing also keeps promises of judgment. Israel's future would hinge on their choice of faithfulness or forgetfulness.

A covenant renewal at Shechem (24:1–13)

Joshua's second farewell address took place at Shechem, the site of Abraham's first altar (Gen. 12:6–7) and the earlier covenant renewal under Joshua (8:30–35). The setting itself reminded Israel of God's enduring faithfulness from generation to generation.

Joshua began by recounting the nation's entire history from Abraham to the conquest, but he did so from God's perspective: "Thus says the Lord, the God of Israel." Every sentence began with divine initiative: "I took your father Abraham," "I gave him Isaac," "I sent Moses," "I plagued Egypt," "I brought you out," "I gave you a land on which you had not labored" (24:3–13). The repetition of "I" underscored God's sovereign grace. Israel's story was not about their achievements but about the Lord's mercy.

By summarizing the nation's history, Joshua reminded them that their identity rested on God's action. The covenant was built on grace, not merit. Their only fitting response was gratitude and loyalty. Israel's past testified that every blessing came from the Lord's faithfulness.

"Choose this day whom you will serve" (24:14–18)

After rehearsing God's goodness, Joshua presented the people with a decisive challenge: "Now therefore fear the Lord and serve him in sincerity and in faithfulness. Put away the gods that your fathers served beyond the River and in Egypt, and serve the Lord" (24:14). The call to fear and serve emphasized reverence and devotion. God's past grace demanded present obedience.

Then came one of the most memorable declarations in Scripture: "And if it is evil in your eyes to serve the Lord, choose this day whom you will serve ... But as for me and my house, we will serve the Lord" (24:15). Joshua's example modeled personal responsibility and leadership. Even if the nation wavered, he would remain steadfast. Faith must begin at home.

The people responded with affirmation: "Far be it from us that we should forsake the Lord to serve other gods" (24:16). They recounted God's mighty acts—deliverance from Egypt, preservation in the wilderness, and victory in Canaan—and pledged their allegiance: "We also will serve the Lord, for he is our God" (24:18). Their confession was sincere but would later be tested.

A covenant confirmed (24:19-28)

Joshua, knowing the frailty of human devotion, warned them again: "You are not able to serve the Lord, for he is a holy God. He is a jealous God; he will not forgive your transgressions or your sins" (24:19). His purpose was not to discourage but to awaken seriousness. True service required holiness and exclusive loyalty. Israel could not treat God lightly or worship him alongside idols.

The people insisted, "No, but we will serve the Lord." Joshua then called them to accountability: "Then put away the foreign gods that are among you, and incline your heart to the Lord, the God of Israel" (24:23). When they renewed their commitment, Joshua formalized it: "So Joshua made a covenant with the people that day, and put in place statutes and rules for them at Shechem" (24:25).

He wrote these words in the Book of the Law and set up a large stone under the oak near the sanctuary. "Behold, this stone shall be a witness against us, for it has heard all the words of the Lord that he spoke to us" (24:27). The stone, like the altar in chapter 22, served as a tangible reminder of covenant faithfulness. Memory was again the safeguard of obedience.

Joshua's death and legacy (24:29-33)

The book closes with the death of Joshua at age 110. "They buried him in his own inheritance at Timnath-serah" (24:30). Two additional burials follow—that of Joseph's bones, carried from Egypt and laid in Shechem (24:32), and that of Eleazar the priest (24:33). These closing verses tie together Israel's past and present. The promise to the patriarchs was fulfilled; the leaders who guided them to that fulfillment had completed their work.

Joshua's life embodied faithfulness from beginning to end. His courage, obedience, and humility set a pattern for every generation of believers. He began as Moses' servant, became Israel's leader, and died as God's faithful witness. The land was conquered, the covenant renewed, and the people reminded to choose the Lord continually.

Theological reflections

Joshua 23–24 brings the book to its fitting conclusion, revealing the heart of covenant faith. First, ***memory sustains obedience***. Joshua's repeated appeals to "remember" show that faith falters when gratitude fades. Recalling God's faithfulness strengthens loyalty in times of temptation.

Second, ***faith demands a choice***. Israel could not serve both God and idols. Joshua's call—"Choose this day"—echoes through every generation. Faith is not inherited but decided. Each believer must personally affirm allegiance to the Lord.

Third, ***leadership begins at home***. Joshua's declaration—"As for me and my house, we will serve the Lord"—places spiritual responsibility first within the family. Godly homes anchor faithful communities.

Fourth, ***covenant faithfulness requires exclusive devotion***. The holiness of God leaves no room for divided hearts. Compromise leads to ruin; consecration leads to rest.

Finally, ***God's faithfulness endures beyond his servants***. Though Joshua, Joseph, and Eleazar died, God's promises continued. The story of Joshua ends not with an ending but with a legacy—faith that endures from generation to generation.

APPLICATION

1. Remembering God's faithfulness fuels obedience

Joshua reminded Israel of all God had done—from delivering them out of Egypt to giving them the land of promise. Memory was not sentimental; it was spiritual. Forgetfulness breeds disobedience, but remembrance produces devotion. Christians likewise must rehearse God's faithfulness often—through Scripture, prayer, and worship. The Lord has proven himself again and again, yet our hearts easily drift when gratitude fades. Every act of obedience begins with a clear memory of grace. When we remember who God is and what he has done, we will be eager to trust him again. Gratitude sustains perseverance. Like Joshua's generation, Christians must learn to look back with thanksgiving so they can move forward in faithfulness. God's past mercies are the surest guarantees of his future grace. To remember well is to remain faithful.

2. Faith requires a personal and daily choice

Joshua's challenge—"Choose this day whom you will serve"—confronts every believer. Faith is not inherited, automatic, or occasional; it is a deliberate and continuing decision to follow the Lord. Each generation must choose afresh, and each day calls for renewed commitment. The idols of our age—comfort, ambition, approval—still compete for the heart's allegiance. The question remains: whom will we serve? Joshua's example begins at home: "As for me and my house, we will serve the Lord." His leadership was grounded in personal conviction and family devotion. The call to choose is not coercion but invitation—the God who saves also calls us to loyalty. True discipleship demands daily resolve: turning from self to Christ, from compromise to conviction. Every sunrise renews the choice to serve the Lord wholeheartedly.

3. God's holiness demands exclusive devotion

Joshua warned Israel that God is holy and jealous—a consuming fire who will not share his glory with idols. His warning was not harsh but loving. God's holiness protects his people from the ruin of divided hearts. Christians today face the same temptation to blend worship with worldliness, to serve God outwardly while harboring competing loyalties within. But covenant faith leaves no room for rivals. The Lord will not be one among many; he must be Lord of all. Holiness requires wholehearted devotion—obedience in both private and public life. Grace does not excuse sin; it empowers holiness. Just as Israel was told to put away foreign gods, believers must continually cast off whatever distracts from faithful service. God's holiness is not a barrier to joy—it is the foundation of it. To serve him alone is to live in peace.

4. God's faithfulness outlasts every generation

Joshua's death closed a chapter in Israel's history, but not in God's story. The burial of Joshua, Joseph, and Eleazar reminded Israel that human leaders pass, yet God's covenant remains. The same Lord who kept his promises to Abraham and Moses would continue guiding his people long after Joshua was gone. Christians can take comfort in this truth: our faith rests not in human strength but in divine permanence. God's purposes outlive his servants. Our calling is to be faithful in our generation, trusting that the next will find the same God faithful still. The church must build on this foundation—passing on truth, teaching Scripture, and modeling obedience so that faith continues after we are gone. The Lord's work never ends with us; his promises endure forever.

CONCLUSION

The story of Joshua closes not with a battle, but with a choice. Israel stood in the land God had promised, surrounded by blessings that testified to his faithfulness. Yet the future depended on one thing—continued loyalty to the Lord. Joshua's challenge, "Choose this day whom you will serve," remains timeless. Faith is not inherited; it must be embraced anew by every heart and home.

Joshua's declaration—"As for me and my house, we will serve the Lord"—was both personal and public. It expressed the conviction that obedience begins in the home and spreads outward. Even after his death, his legacy endured because his faith was rooted in remembrance and obedience. The book of Joshua ends where all faithful lives must: resting in the promises of a God who never fails and serving him with undivided hearts.

REFLECTION

1. Why did Joshua remind Israel of God's past faithfulness before calling them to obedience?

2. What idols or distractions most threaten your loyalty to God today?

3. How does Joshua's example challenge you to lead your home in faith?

4. What does it mean to "serve the Lord in sincerity and faithfulness"?

5. How can remembering God's promises strengthen you to resist compromise?

6. What legacy of faith do you hope to leave for the next generation?

DISCUSSION

1. Why is it significant that Joshua's final appeal centered on choice rather than command?

2. How does Joshua's covenant renewal at Shechem mirror the church's commitment to Christ?

3. What does this passage teach about the relationship between grace, memory, and obedience?

4. Why did Joshua warn the people that serving God would not be easy?

5. How can believers today renew their covenant with God in practical ways?

6. What truths from Joshua's life summarize the message of the entire book?

www.ingramcontent.com/pod-product-compliance
Lightning Source LLC
Chambersburg PA
CBHW070153080526
44586CB00015B/1971